WOMEN SCIENTISTS AND ENGINEERS EMPLOYED IN INDUSTRY

Why So Few?

A Report Based on a Conference

Ad hoc Panel on Industry

Committee on Women in Science and Engineering

Office of Scientific and Engineering Personnel

National Research Council

NATIONAL ACADEMY PRESS
Washington, D.C.   1994

Library of Congress Catalog Card No. 93-86930
International Standard Book Number 0-309-04991-1

Additional copies of this report are available from:
National Academy Press
2101 Constitution Avenue, NW——Box 285
Washington, DC 20055

B-263

COMMITTEE ON WOMEN
IN SCIENCE AND ENGINEERING

‡JEWEL PLUMMER COBB, President and Professor Emerita, California State University–Fullerton, and Trustee Professor, California State University–Los Angeles, *Chair*

‡CHARLOTTE V. KUH, Executive Director of the Graduate Record Examinations Program, Educational Testing Service, *Vice-Chair*

*BETSY ANCKER-JOHNSON, Chair, World Environment Center, and Vice-president, General Motors Corporation, Environmental Activities (retired)

*GEORGE CAMPBELL JR., President, National Action Council for Minorities in Engineering

‡NANCY E. CANTOR, Professor and Chair, Department of Psychology, Princeton University

*†ESTHER M. CONWELL, Research Fellow, Xerox Corporation, *Vice-Chair*

*†MILDRED S. DRESSELHAUS, Institute Professor of Electrical Engineering and Physics, Massachusetts Institute of Technology, *Chair*

CAROLA EISENBERG, Lecturer in psychiatry and Dean of Student Affairs, Harvard Medical School (retired)

‡LOUIS A. FERNANDEZ, Dean, School of Natural Sciences, California State University–San Bernardino

†BRUCE ANDREW FOWLER, Director of the Toxicology Program, University of Maryland Medical School

---

* Member of the Ad Hoc Panel on Industry.
† Term ended in 1993.
‡ Term began in 1993.

†LILLI S. HORNIG, Visiting Research Scholar, Center for Research on Women, Wellesley College

*†PAT HILL HUBBARD, Senior Vice-president of Public Affairs, American Electronics Association

*SHIRLEY A. JACKSON, Professor of Physics, Rutgers University

‡WILLIE PEARSON, JR., Professor of Sociology, Wake Forest University

†GIAN-CARLO ROTA, Professor of Applied Mathematics and Philosophy, Massachusetts Institute of Technology

†GARRISON SPOSITO, Professor of Soil Physical Chemistry, University of California—Berkeley

‡LOIS STEELE, Research Medical Officer, Indian Health Service—Tucson

KAREN K. UHLENBECK, Professor of Mathematics, University of Texas—Austin

NRC Staff:
Linda C. Skidmore, Staff Officer
Gaelyn Davidson, Administrative Assistant

---

* Member of the Ad Hoc Panel on Industry.
† Term ended in 1993.
‡ Term began in 1993.

v

ACKNOWLEDGMENTS

The Committee on Women in Science and Engineering (CWSE) is a continuing committee within the National Research Council's Office of Scientific and Engineering Personnel. The goal of the Committee is to increase the participation of women in science and engineering by convening meetings, conducting research, and disseminating data about the status of women in these fields. The Committee's core activities are funded by a consortium of federal and private organizations. For their roles in securing contributions of partial funding for the core activities of the Committee, their sharing with the Committee the concerns of their organizations relevant to the Committee's mandate, and their participation in the Committee's deliberations about topics that it might examine in order to address the underparticipation of women in science and engineering, we are grateful to the following sponsor representatives: Bruce Guile, National Academy of Engineering; Harriet Zuckerman, Andrew W. Mellon Foundation; Charles R. Bowen, International Business Machines Corporation; Mark Myers, Xerox Corporation; Burton H. Colvin, National Institute for Standards and Technology; Marguerite Hays and Ted Lorei, Department of Veterans Affairs; Roosevelt Calbert and Lola Rogers, National Science Foundation; Sherri McGee, National Aeronautics and Space Administration; Sheila Rosenthal, U.S. Environmental Protection Agency; and Cindy Musick, U.S. Department of Energy's Office of Energy Research. Finally, we recognize the financial support given by the General Electric Foundation, Battelle Pacific Northwest Laboratories, and the National Research Council, specifically for the conference, "Women Scientists and Engineers Employed in Industry: Why So Few?"

Oversight for the conference and this report was provided by a group of CWSE members having a wide range of experience in industry: Betsy Ancker-Johnson, George Campbell, Jr., Esther Conwell, Mildred S. Dresselhaus, and Shirley A. Jackson. We especially acknowledge the efforts of two individuals: Dr. Conwell, conference chair, and Dr. Dresselhaus, CWSE chair, devoted much time reviewing the manuscripts during the first six months of 1993.

The Committee on Women in Science and Engineering publicly acknowledges the thoughtful contributions of the 150 participants at the conference held on January 17-18, 1993. Although they are not listed in this report, these individuals—women practicing science and engineering in the industrial work force of the United States, managers in that technological work force, human resources staff at companies ranging from small businesses to Fortune 500 corporations, and researchers investigating the underparticipation of women in science and engineering in general and the science and engineering (S&E) industrial work force in particular—shared experiences, without which this report could not have been developed. Furthermore, we applaud the meritorious efforts of the five companies described in some detail in Chapter III, also recognizing that still other U.S. companies have undertaken programs to enhance the participation of women in their technological work forces. It is the Committee's intention to continue to disseminate information about such programs exhibiting effectiveness in recruiting women and advancing their careers in science and engineering.

Finally, the Committee is indebted to the staff of the National Research Council's Office of Scientific and Engineering Personnel for providing the forum and creating the environment in which its initial examination of the status of industrially employed women scientists and engineers could occur. Throughout this project—from initial planning of the conference through dissemination of this report—activities have been coordinated competently by the CWSE study director, Linda C. Skidmore. Pamela Ebert Flattau, director of studies and surveys, offered valuable advice during the planning of the conference. Judy Scott wrote a summary of the 2-day conference, which formed the basis of this report. Gaelyn Davidson, administrative assistant, handled conference logistics and most word processing for this report.

The contributions of these many individuals and organizations have resulted in this first CWSE volume looking at the status of women scientists and engineers employed in the industrial sector of the United States. One recommendation during the final plenary session of the January 1993 conference was for the Committee to hold a series of conferences at which this issue would continue to be examined. The Committee has begun to act on that recommendation, with the endorsement of the National Research Council's Office of Scientific and Engineering Personnel and the Executive Committee of the Council's Governing Board. The Committee is grateful for the continued support of the National Research Council, as evidenced by this recent action.

CONTENTS

LIST OF FIGURES

xi

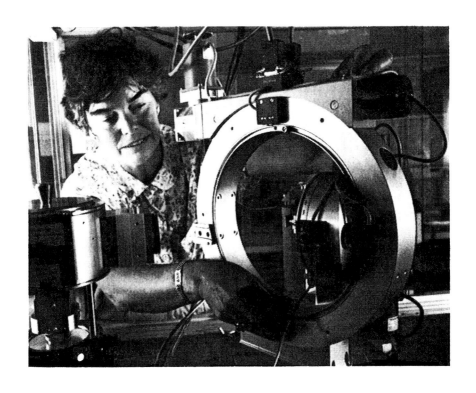

Using X-ray diffraction analysis, Joka Vandenberg evaluates the quality of layered crystals used in making strained-multi-quantum-well lasers. (Photo: AT&T Bell Laboratories)

EXECUTIVE SUMMARY

Women comprise about 12 percent of the employed scientific and engineering (S&E) labor force in industry. While this is due in part to the specific subfields selected by women, another significant contributing factor is the attrition rate for women scientists and engineers in industry, which is double that for men and substantially higher than for other employment sectors. These compelling facts led the Committee on Women in Science and Engineering (CWSE) of the National Research Council to plan a conference, "Women Scientists and Engineers Employed in Industry: Why So Few?," to examine the workplace environment for women pursuing careers in industry. The conference provided a forum for women scientists and engineers to share data and personal experiences to uncover the principal causes of underrepresentation of S&E women in industry and to explore effective strategies for change. In addition, representatives of five companies having established exemplary programs to recruit and retain women scientists and engineers——Aerospace Corporation, ALCOA, AT&T Bell Laboratories, Xerox Corporate Research and Technology, and Scios Nova——described strategies proven to be effective in removing barriers for women scientists and engineers.

Limited access is the first hurdle faced by women seeking industrial jobs in science and engineering. While progress has been made in this area in recent years, common recruitment and hiring practices that make extensive use of traditional networks often overlook the available pool of women. Once on the job, many women find paternalism, sexual harassment, allegations of reverse discrimination, different standards for judging the work of men and women, lower salary relative to their male peers, inequitable job assignments, and other aspects of a male-oriented culture that are hostile to women. Women to a greater extent than men find limited opportunities for advancement, particularly for moving into management positions. The number of women who have achieved the top levels in corporations is much lower than would be expected, based on the pipeline model.

Conferees agreed that attention to work-family issues is of paramount importance for retention of women scientists and engineers. Other important measures to improve the environment for women are mentoring and the establishment of women's networks.

The initiatives for improving the climate for women taken by the five companies noted above had many common elements, the most important being chief executive officer support. Other elements included availability of

1

flexible work schedules, part-time employment, and parental leave programs; involvement in providing or recommending day-care facilities; and counseling programs. Career development was facilitated by clarification of the criteria for promotion and by efforts to increase mobility through lateral transfers. Evaluation by some companies has shown that initiatives such as these yield measurable improvements in the retention of women.

Given the issues faced by women scientists and engineers in industry, an important component of the conference was to identify effective strategies for succeeding in a technological career in the industrial employment sector. In particular, conference participants considered the attributes and strategies of women scientists and engineers who had succeeded. These women, above all, have excellent technical skills and are self-confident, able to establish clear goals, and comfortable taking risks. They communicate well and are open to change, particularly in the area of professional growth. Women managers must have, in addition to these qualities, a feeling of empowerment, a "can-do" attitude, and a commitment to helping others. Not surprisingly, these are also the attributes of successful men.

Many people have questioned the advisability of encouraging women to go into S&E careers at a time when there are few job openings in some fields. Conferees agreed that, particularly in difficult times, it is essential for companies to have the most talented people, whatever their gender or race. Clearly the essential recommendations that emerged from the conference that will benefit women will also benefit men and will be critical to the health of the corporate sector.

Maria Isabel Soto uses a scanning electron microscope to find defects in an electrical circuit.
(Photo: The Aerospace Corporation)

Bob Opila and Amy Muller prepare a scanning Auger microprobe for analysis.
(Photo: AT&T Bell Laboratories)

I. THE REPRESENTATION OF WOMEN SCIENTISTS AND ENGINEERS IN INDUSTRY

In this chapter we introduce a statistical base for the descriptions of the industrial environment confronted by women scientists and engineers that appear in subsequent chapters. It summarizes the relatively low rate of participation by these women in industrial settings and examines the origins of this rate. Subsequent chapters enrich this statistical summary by illuminating through personal experiences one of the possible reasons for the low rate of participation——a perception that the work environment in industry is particularly inhospitable to female scientists and engineers.

Although women comprised 16 percent of the U.S. scientific and engineering (S&E) labor force in 1988, they represented only 12.3 percent (or roughly 400,000) of the scientists and engineers employed in industry that year.[1] The relatively low representation of women scientists and engineers in industry, as well as the fact that more quantitative data are available on academic rather than industrial employment in the United States, motivated the conference held by the National Research Council's Committee on Women in Science and Engineering (CWSE) in January 1993.[2] The statistics underlying the question "Why so few?" are examined in this chapter. They focus on three aspects of the education and employment of women during the past few decades:

(1)   the lower percentage of women earning S&E[3] degrees, at all levels;

---

[1] National Science Foundation, *U.S. Scientists and Engineers: 1988* (NSF 89-322), Washington, DC: NSF, 1989, Table B-7. The 1986 figure is the most recent released by NSF to describe the characteristics of the employed labor force by sector and gender. The numbers reported by NSF for industry exclude self-employed scientists and engineers.

[2] For instance, *Science & Engineering Indicators: 1991,* the most recent of this biennial series from the National Science Board, reveals the numbers of industrially employed scientists and engineers but does not disaggregate that data by gender.

[3] S&E includes the physical, mathematical, computer, environmental, life, and social sciences; psychology; and engineering.

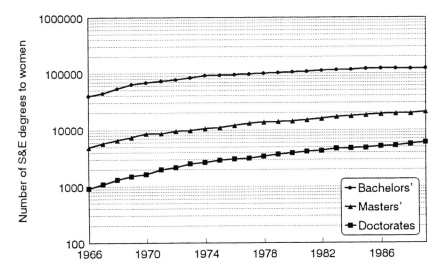

NOTE: The ordinate is a logarithmic scale.
SOURCE: National Science Foundation, *Science and Engineering Degrees: 1966-89 (A Source Book)* (NSF 91-314), Washington, DC: NSF, 1991.

Figure I-1. Number of science and engineering (S&E) degrees awarded to women, by degree level, 1966-1989.

(2)   the specific S&E disciplines in which women tend to earn degrees being less important, on average, for industrial employment; and

(3)   the lower likelihood for women in a given field to choose industrial employment.

In large part, the small number of women scientists and engineers employed in industry reflects the small total number of women scientists and engineers in the employed work force. In 1986 only 15 percent (or roughly 700,000) of the employed S&E labor force was female.[4] Thus, a large part

---

[4] NSF, *op. cit.* Within that 15 percent, 10 percent of employed women scientists and engineers are minority women (see George Campbell Jr, and R. A. Ellis, *Minorities in Engineering* (Manpower Bulletin 110), Washington, DC: American Association of Engineering Societies Inc., 1991).

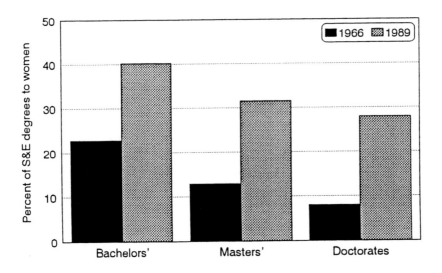

SOURCE: National Science Foundation, *Science and Engineering Degrees: 1966-89 (A Source Book)* (NSF 91-314), Washington, DC: NSF, 1991.

Figure I-2. Percentage of science and engineering (S&E) degrees awarded to women, by degree level, 1966 and 1989.

of the answer to the question "Why so few?" originates in the lower participation in the past of women in the S&E education pipeline and, subsequently, in careers.

This part of the answer to "Why so few?" can be expected to become less important in the future, however, since women have been increasing their representation in S&E education. Figure I-1 illustrates this trend. At the bachelor's and master's degree levels, the number increased by more than fourfold; at the doctorate level, the increase was more than sixfold from 1966 levels.

The net result of these dramatic increases has been that the percentage of female degree recipients as a share of all S&E degree recipients increased significantly (Figure I-2). In 1966 women constituted less than 24 percent of the S&E bachelor's degree recipients, less than 14 percent of the S&E master's degree recipients, and 8 percent of the S&E doctorate recipients. By 1989 the percentage of S&E degrees awarded to women had increased dramatically at all degree levels——to 40 percent, 31 percent, and

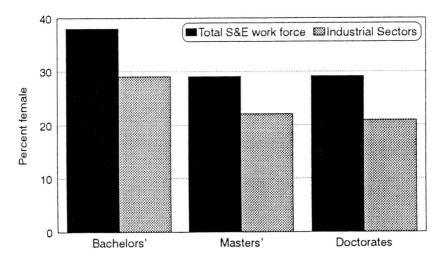

SOURCES: National Science Foundation, *Characteristics of Recent Science and Engineering Graduates: 1990* (NSF 92-316), Washington, DC: NSF, 1992; Delores H. Thurgood and Joanne M. Weinman, *Summary Report 1990: Doctorate Recipients from United States Universities*, Washington, DC: National Academy Press, 1991.

Figure I-3. Women as a percentage of the total science and engineering (S&E) and industrial S&E employment pools, by degree level, 1990.

28 percent, respectively, indicating also an increase in relative probability for receiving advanced degrees.[5]

Despite this growth, however, female scientists and engineers remain underrepresented in industry, partly because of their choice of S&E field and partly because of their choice of employment sector. Figure I-3 shows that, at all degree levels (B.S., M.S., and Ph.D.), the percentage of female S&E degree recipients entering the total S&E work force (38 percent B.S., 28 percent M.S., and 28 percent Ph.D.) was significantly higher than the corresponding percentages of female S&E degree recipients entering industrial positions (28 percent B.S., 22 percent M.S., 21 percent Ph.D.).

---

[5] Although representation of women has increased dramatically at all levels, women continue to represent a declining fraction of S&E degree recipients at each successive level.

In part this is because women tend less to enter S&E fields likely to lead to industrial employment, but even after taking into account field preference, there is evidence that for most fields the share of women in industry is still below the comparable share for men. At the baccalaureate level the industrial share of employment was lower for women in five out of eight broad fields: mathematical, computer, life, behavioral, and social sciences. These five fields represented about three-fourths of the 1990 female S&E employment (Table I-1). Similar findings result at the master's degree level, where the share for women was less in six fields representing almost 90 percent of 1990 female S&E employment (Table I-2).

The findings for doctorates (Table I-3) is even more striking. Except for environmental sciences, a relatively small field, the industrial share of employment was small for women in all fields.

These findings indicate that part of the answer to the question "Why so few?" must come from factors other than the simple scarcity of women from S&E careers.

As noted earlier, one of these factors is the tendency for female scientists and engineers to choose careers in life sciences, behavioral sciences, and social sciences, fields in which industry is a less likely source of employment than academe or government (Figure I-4). In 1989 three-fourths of the S&E bachelor's degrees awarded to women were in these three fields. In contrast, only about 46 percent of the S&E bachelor's degrees awarded to men were in these fields. Similar patterns are observed among the S&E degree recipients at the master's and doctorate levels.

The degree to which industry is a relatively less important source of employment for these fields than for the physical sciences and engineering is shown in Tables I-1 to I-3 and in Figure I-5. Sixty-two percent of the 1988 and 1989 employed S&E bachelor's degree recipients had jobs in industry in 1990. In contrast, only 46 percent of the degree recipients in the life sciences had such jobs. The share was 44 percent in the behavioral sciences and 59 percent in the social sciences. Again, the S&E degree recipients at the master's and doctorate levels show similar patterns, although the absolute numbers and percentages employed in industry are smaller than at the bachelor's level.

The fact that women tend to prefer jobs in other sectors is consistent with a perception that working conditions for women are less favorable in industry. It may also be consistent with a number of other hypotheses, however, some of which involve decisions based on factors other than the nature of working conditions in industry.

9

TABLE I-1: 1988 and 1989 Science and Engineering (S&E) Bachelor's Degree Recipients[a] Employed in Industry[b] in 1990 (as a percentage of recent graduates in all sectors): All employed graduates and female and male graduates, by field

Selected Fields	All S&E Workers		Female S&E Workers		Male S&E Workers	
	Number in Thousands	Percent in Industry	Number in Thousands	Percent in Industry	Number in Thousands	Percent in Industry
All S&E fields[c]	484.6	62.1	186.4	49.0	298.2	70.3
All sciences:						
Physical sciences	16.5	60.6	5.3	64.2	11.2	56.3
Mathematical sciences	26.6	53.4	13.0	48.5	13.6	58.1
Computer sciences	62.1	78.8	16.7	77.8	45.4	79.1
Environmental sciences	4.7	61.7	1.2	66.7	3.5	60.0
Life sciences	69.2	46.0	34.7	42.3	34.5	49.6
Behavioral sciences	63.3	43.6	44.0	37.3	19.3	58.0
Social sciences	115.8	58.8	52.7	55.0	63.1	62.0
All engineering	126.6	76.7	18.7	77.5	107.9	76.6

[a] Considered "recent graduates" in 1990.
[b] Excluding from industrial employment those S&E recipients who reported self-employment.
[c] Numbers may not add due to rounding.
SOURCE: National Science Foundation (NSF), *Characteristics of Recent S&E Graduates: 1990* (NSF 92-316), Washington, DC: NSF, 1990, Tables B-6 and B-26.

TABLE I-2: 1988 and 1989 Science and Engineering (S&E) Master's Degree Recipients[a] Employed in Industry[b] in 1990 (as a percentage of the recent S&E graduates in all sectors): All employed graduates and female and male graduates, by field

Selected Fields	All S&E Workers		Female S&E Workers		Male S&E Workers	
	Number in Thousands	Percent in Industry	Number in Thousands	Percent in Industry	Number in Thousands	Percent in Industry
All S&E fields[c]	100.4	57.7	29.6	42.4	70.8	64.0
All sciences:						
Physical sciences	5.1	54.9	1.4	57.1	3.7	54.1
Mathematical sciences	8.4	40.5	3.4	35.3	5.0	44.0
Computer sciences	19.4	75.3	5.1	78.4	14.3	74.8
Environmental sciences	4.0	57.5	1.1	54.5	2.9	58.6
Life sciences	11.7	27.4	5.7	17.5	6.0	36.7
Behavioral sciences	4.5	33.3	2.8	32.1	1.7	35.3
Social sciences	13.4	30.6	5.8	24.1	7.6	35.5
All engineering	33.8	77.2	4.2	69.0	29.6	78.4

[a] Considered "recent graduates" in 1990.
[b] Excluding from industrial employment those S&E recipients who reported self-employment.
[c] Numbers may not add due to rounding.

SOURCE: National Science Foundation (NSF), Characteristics of Recent S&E Graduates: 1990 (NSF 92-316), Washington, DC: NSF, 1990, Tables B-6 and B-26.

TABLE I-3: 1988 and 1989 Science and Engineering (S&E) Ph.D. Recipients Employed in Industry[a] in 1990 (as a percentage of recent S&E Ph.D.s in all sectors): All employed Ph.D.s and female and male Ph.D.s, by field

Selected Fields	All S&E Workers		Female S&E Workers		Male S&E Workers	
	Number in Thousands	Percent in Industry	Number in Thousands	Percent in Industry	Number in Thousands	Percent in Industry
All S&E fields[b]	37.7	24.4	11.7	15.0	26.0	28.7
All sciences:	30.7	18.2	11.0	13.3	19.7	20.9
Physical sciences	5.7	42.9	1.1	53.2	4.6	40.4
Mathematical sciences	1.4	14.7	0.3	4.9	1.0	17.7
Computer sciences	1.1	26.7	0.2	22.9	0.9	27.5
Environmental sciences	1.2	15.8	0.2	22.3	1.0	14.3
Life sciences	10.2	13.6	4.0	9.9	6.1	16.0
Behavioral sciences	5.7	9.3	3.2	6.2	2.5	13.3
Social sciences	5.5	10.1	2.0	9.1	3.5	10.6
All engineering	7.0	52.0	0.7	42.8	6.3	53.0

[a] Excluding from industrial employment those recipients who reported self-employment.
[b] Numbers may not add due to rounding.
SOURCE: Unpublished data, National Research Council, 1991 Survey of Doctorate Recipients.

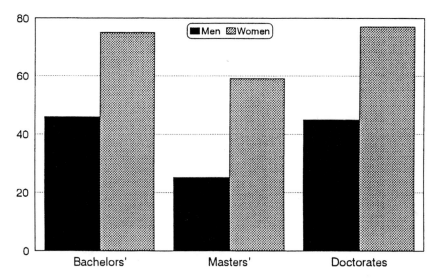

SOURCE: National Science Foundation, *Science and Engineering Degrees: 1966-89 (A Source Book)* (NSF 91-314), Washington, DC: NSF, 1991.

Figure I-4. Percentage of women and men receiving degrees in life, behavioral, and social sciences, by degree level, 1989.

Another fact consistent with the working conditions explanation is the greater exit rate of women than men from S&E positions in industry. Here again, the results may be consistent with other hypotheses. Using survey data from the National Science Foundation (NSF) and with support from NSF and the Alfred P. Sloan Foundation, Anne Preston of the State University of New York at Stony Brook has been investigating the exit rate of women from the natural sciences and engineering after they have been educated and employed in those fields. The results of this survey[6] showed

---

[6] Anne Preston, "A Study of Occupational Departure of Employees in the Natural Sciences and Engineering," CWSE conference, Irvine, CA, January 17, 1993. This study addressed the question of occupational exit with a number of different data sets and methodologies. The first data set was a national study of occupational exit rates of men and women during the 1980s, using data collected by NSF from about 80,000 male and female

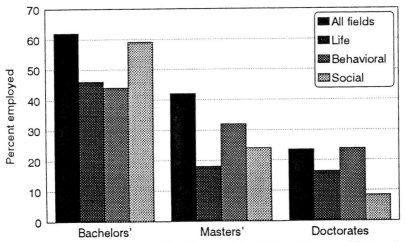

SOURCES: National Science Foundation, *Characteristics of Recent Science and Engineering Graduates: 1990* (NSF 92-316), Washington, DC: NSF, 1992; Delores H. Thurgood and Joanne M. Weinman, *Summary Report 1990: Doctorate Recipients from United States Universities,* Washington, DC: National Academy Press, 1991.

Figure I-5. Percentage of 1988 and 1989 science and engineering (S&E) degree recipients employed in industry, by degree level, total and selected fields, 1990.

that over the 7-year period, 1982 to 1989, women's exit rates from S&E jobs were roughly twice as high as men's exit rates. In addition, of the women employed in science and engineering in 1982, 20 percent had left by 1989. Interestingly, as shown in Figure I-6, there was also a big difference in the exit rates of women in industry and women in the public and nonprofit

---

scientists and engineers between 1982 and 1989. The second set of data was obtained from a survey of 1,450 women and men—all degreed graduates in either math, science, or engineering—at a public university in the Northeast. Third, from the survey responses, 50 women—paired on the basis of similarities in terms of age, education, field of study, and family characteristics—participated in in-depth interviews; the difference between the two women within each pair was that one had left science and one had stayed.

14

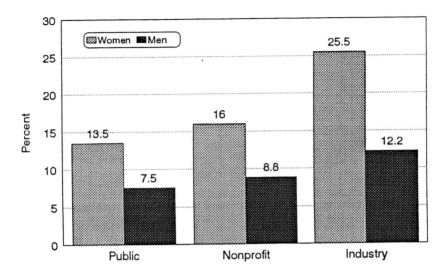

SOURCES: Anne Preston, "A Study of Occupational Departure of Employees in the Natural Sciences and Engineering," CWSE conference, Irvine, CA, January 17, 1993.

Figure I-6. Male and female exit rate, by sector (percentage of scientists and engineers employed in 1982 who had left S&E employment by 1989).

employment sectors. Over the 7-year period, the exit rate of women in industry was almost twice the exit rate of women in government.

    With reference to the data for men, the Preston study revealed that 7.5 percent of male scientists and engineers employed by the government, 8.8 percent of those employed in the nonprofit sector, and 12.2 percent of those employed in private industry in 1982 had left S&E jobs by 1989. As with women, of the three sectors, the rate of exit of men was largest in private industry. However, while women in private industry were almost twice as likely as women in government to leave S&E jobs, men in industry were roughly 1.6 times more likely than men in government to leave S&E employment.

    It is noteworthy that exit rates for Ph.D. women from all employment sectors were smaller, in fact comparable to the rates for men. Further results from this study will be given in Chapter II.

Organization of the Report

In summary, although the major factor that determines the size of the industrial S&E work force is an individual's selection of a particular degree field, gender differences persist even after field choice is controlled for. One possible explanation for these residual differences is the perception of a less favorable climate for women in industry. The profound implications of this possible perception led the Committee on Women in Science and Engineering to hold a conference to examine the relevant issues. The report of the conference follows. Chapter II addresses aspects of the corporate culture that may create perceptions of an inhospitable work environment in industry for women scientists and engineers. Subsequent chapters describe actions taken by both corporate employers (Chapter III) and women scientists and engineers themselves (Chapter IV) to facilitate the entry and retention of women in the nation's technological work force. Finally, the Committee's conclusions are summarized in Chapter V.

II. BARRIERS FOR WOMEN IN CORPORATE CULTURE

The apparent preference of women scientists and engineers for jobs outside the industrial sector and the larger exit rate of women than men from industrial employment suggest that women perceive the climate in industry as less than favorable for a scientific or technical career. Conference participants identified a number of underlying causes of this apparent inhospitable climate for women. Barriers that inhibit progress for women scientists and engineers in industry were found at every stage of career development:

- recruitment and hiring practices that create *de facto* entry barriers for women,
- aspects of a male-oriented corporate culture that are hostile to women,
- paternalism,
- allegations of reverse discrimination,
- sexual harassment,
- different standards for women and men,
- disparities in the distribution of high-quality job assignments,
- salary discrepancies based on one's sex,
- failure of corporations to accommodate work-family issues, and
- difficulty for women to advance into management.

In this chapter we define these barriers, present evidence of their persistence in corporations, and review the understanding that emerged at the conference of their impact on women. In particular, we focus on institutional or cultural attributes of corporations that (1) limit access of women to jobs, (2) create less than favorable working conditions for women, and (3) lead to high attrition rates for women in industry. Later chapters will examine corporate initiatives aimed at neutralizing these negative factors and will offer strategies that can help women overcome them.

Access

Recognizing the advantages inherent in utilizing women scientists and engineers in the corporate labor force, a number of companies——for

17

instance, E. I. duPont de Nemours and Company——have developed aggressive programs and strategies to recruit more women into these fields:

> Strength gained from diversity is the goal of our affirmative action program. Since projections of the future work force indicate that 80-85 percent of net additions over the next 10 years will be minorities and women, [greater] diversity is inevitable. The vision is to manage this to our advantage. We must recruit aggressively among these groups or the best and brightest will go elsewhere. We must train and develop our employees to get full use of their talents and capabilities. If we accomplish this, DuPont can continue to be one of the world's leading industrial companies. . . .[7]

Other companies were forced to open their doors to women in science and engineering by federal affirmative action policies initiated in the 1970s. While some programs have been effective, yielding significant progress in recent years, barriers that limit access to industry jobs for women remain.

The rapidly changing work environment in corporations today, coupled with internal competition for head count (i.e., full-time employees), creates pressures to fill jobs quickly. Consequently, positions are often not advertised externally, and employers resort to traditional recruiting and hiring practices, using well-established and often exclusive networks. Women are not as likely to be well represented (firmly rooted) in these networks, which include internal and external personal contacts and linkages with search firms.

Personal experiences shared at the conference illuminate some of the problems. According to one Ph.D. microbiologist, her first employer, in 1977, decided to begin hiring women only under threat of legal action. Six months before she was hired, she believes she would not even have been interviewed:

> In 1977 the company hired seven women at the Ph.D. level; these were added to an existing work force of about 300 people at all levels from the B.S. through the Ph.D. The

---

[7] Robert C. Forney, cited in E. I. dupont de Nemours and Company (hereafter, DuPont), *Diversity: A Source of Strength,* Wilmington, DE: DuPont, 1988.

company was pleased; they had acquired very well-qualified women who were so eager to prove themselves that they did whatever was asked. By 1986, about one-third of the middle level management was women——even though women were less than a third of the work force overall—— because women had demonstrated they had the very skills the company was looking for. However, it is important to keep in mind that the company would never have known this if it had not been forced by law to hire women.[8]

In general, traditional recruiting and hiring practices were not consciously designed to exclude women. Nevertheless, they embody a predilection for replicating the attributes of the existing work force. In a small but growing manufacturing company where one conference participant is employed, managers responding to the question "Why haven't we hired more women?" answered:

- "We choose the best person."
- "The person must fit in with the rest of the group."
- "There weren't any women applicants."
- "We need a person who can hit the ground running."
- "The job requires long hours and weekends."

What is the result of these messages? The company has what was referred to as a "model applicant," a stereotyped perception of the ideal candidate. If an applicant fits this model and the perceived comfort level of the group, the person is hired and the group reproduces itself. Often candidates are found when employees call their colleagues at other companies. While the company is thus spared the time and expense of more thorough recruiting, the net effect is reduced access for women, particularly minority women,[9] who usually are not part of that collegial network.

---

[8] Jane S. Allen, presentation at the CWSE conference, Irvine, CA, January 17, 1993.

[9] Rosemary E. Chang, member of the technical staff at Silicon Graphics Computer Systems, presentation at the CWSE conference, Irvine, CA, January 17, 1993.

The Workplace Environment

The atmosphere of the workplace may be one in which women do not feel comfortable. However, subtle aspects of male-oriented culture that are hostile to women can be extremely hard to manage because they are deeply ingrained and because their impact is difficult to demonstrate.

Marion Yuen, director of advisory services for Catalyst,[10] reported findings from a 1991 study of female engineers employed in 30 large corporations, ranging from aerospace and chemical utilities to manufacturers of consumer products and high technology. She noted,

> Catalyst has spent many years studying working women, but seldom have research participants been as vocal about the nature of their work experiences——it is clear that female engineers really like the nature of what they do. As they enthusiastically discuss their work, they also share with us the difficult working conditions they encounter.[11]

Among the working conditions reported by Catalyst as inhibiting female engineers' productivity and retarding the development of their full potential——and supported in statements by both engineers and scientists at the CWSE-sponsored conference——were paternalism, sexual harassment, and the pressures associated with peers' allegations of reverse

---

[10] Catalyst is a nonprofit organization that works with businesses to effect change for women through research and advisory services and communication.

[11] In this referenced study, focus groups of human resource professionals were convened to guide the lines of inquiry. In addition, focus groups of women and men who were working engineers were also convened, and interviews were conducted with their engineering supervisors. Finally, both working engineers and human resources professionals helped Catalyst to interpret the results.

discrimination.[12] These issues and others, such as the perception of different standards for judging men and women and misunderstandings due to different styles of communication, create a negative workplace environment for women; they are discussed in what follows.

Paternalism

Catalyst's study found that paternalism———that is, condescending or protective treatment of women by men in authority at their companies———continues to be widespread. For instance, even though women may express the desire to be considered for a particular assignment, which may be critical for their professional development, certain work environments are often deemed inappropriate for them because they are women. Sometimes physical strength is assumed to be a necessary attribute for a particular assignment when it is really technological competence and persistence that are important in carrying out the assignment. For example, it was noted at the CWSE conference that some people still treat women geoscientists as though they, more so than male geoscientists, must be protected from the stresses and dangers associated with certain geoscience work———particularly fieldwork involving mines or ocean-going vessels.

Despite the fact that women are willing to take the necessary physical risks or make sacrifices to gain work experience, they are often not offered the opportunity. One human resource representative told Catalyst that there was sometimes a tendency to put women in staff projects because of the perception that they cannot handle themselves in the plant.

A survey of a sample of graduates of Cornell University's School of Engineering found that

> [t]he women interviewed contend that in the critical early stages of women's careers, many older men in management positions tended to assume a paternalistic attitude toward them. One woman's theory was that if you work for someone who coddles you, you tend to live down to those expectations. If someone expects you to accomplish great things, you try to achieve them, learn something from your

---

[12] Catalyst, "Findings from a Study of Women in Engineering," CATALYST *Perspective*, May 1992.

efforts, and build your self-confidence. This paternalistic attitude is especially detrimental to women in companies which, early in their employees' careers, target those with management potential for special career development.[13]

Still another example of paternalism is corporate management's doubts about women's willingness or ability to handle both work and family responsibilities. This disbelief extends, very often, to doubting the future reliability of single women. This paternalistic attitude is not new. As Ehrhart and Sandler reported in their examination of women students in nontraditional fields,

> [t]he devaluation that women face is evident in the perception that women are not as serious about their work. . . . "Why not stop with a B.S.? A pretty girl like you is bound to get married" is an all-too-common refrain. . . . When frequently faced with doubts about their ability and their commitment, many women, not surprisingly, lose self-esteem and career confidence. . . .[14]

Even if these attitudes have no basis in fact, the *perception* of their existence by women scientists and engineers is a fact. Thus, there is a need to establish whether the perception of many of the conference participants reflects reality.

Similarly, some women at the conference felt they were trapped in futile, patronizing relationships in their companies, the kind of relationships that graduate students sometimes have with their advisers. They felt unable to develop their own identities and maturity in the workplace.

---

[13] Deborah Celentano Gerber, presentation at the CWSE conference, Irvine, CA, January 17, 1993.

[14] Julie Kuhn Ehrhart and Bernice R. Sandler, *Looking for More Than a Few Good Women in Traditionally Male Fields*, Washington, DC: American Association of Colleges, Project on the Status and Education of Women, 1987.

Allegations of Reverse Discrimination

A number of conference participants cited the importance of a critical mass of women at the work site in order for individual women to succeed and advance. They noted, however, that, as the numbers of women in the work place grow, men may begin to perceive women and other underrepresented groups to be much stronger and more numerous than they actually are. They may feel threatened, and a backlash against women may occur.

Allegations of reverse discrimination——that is, charges that men are penalized because of special incentives and programs for women——also serve to contribute to a hostile work environment for women scientists and engineers. One female engineer at the conference felt she was being set up for failure by the persistent implication that she had risen to the next level only because she was female. Other conference participants, who had experienced the effects of these allegations both first-hand and indirectly, said that these allegations create or reinforce perceptions by some men and women that women, indeed, do not belong.

One way of combating this notion that women are getting all of the advantages is to provide data; some companies have begun to publish statistics more widely on how opportunities within the company are filled, including lateral transfers, promotions, and so on. More information about such activities is provided in Chapter III.

Sexual Harassment

As noted by Hughes and Sandler, women in nontraditional fields, which include engineering and most fields of science, are among the four groups of women especially vulnerable to sexual harassment "because they may be perceived as 'barging into' an area where women 'don't belong' and should not be in competition with men for jobs."[15] Minority women entering science and engineering (S&E) jobs in industry, it was also pointed out to the Committee, are frequently seen as "economic competitors, new on the scene, highly visible, but not of the 'in' group." Because, as recently as

---

[15] Jean O. Hughes and Bernice R. Sandler, *In Case of Sexual Harassment*, Washington, DC: Association of American Colleges, Project on the Status and Education of Women, 1986.

25 years ago, women were advised to become homemakers, nurses, or precollege teachers, there are many fields considered to be nontraditional for women. Catalyst found that sexual harassment is evidenced, for example, by the posting of pin-ups in the workplace, nuances of language used by male co-workers, and putting the only female engineer at a business meeting on the spot by asking irrelevant, tangential, gender-related questions. For instance, in the Catalyst study, a human resources representative questioned the appropriateness of a particular job for a female engineer, saying,

> The engines will finally fire up at 11:00 at night and . . .
> you've got to be there. . . . That's where heroes are made
> and that's kind of conflicting with family responsibilities.[16]

As employees become more informed about the nature of sexual harassment, both they and their employers may act to eliminate it. For instance, the first class-action sexual-harassment case in U.S. federal courts was settled in May 1993 against a company found "liable for creating a hostile work environment by allowing abusive graffiti and language." The state of Minnesota has sued the same company "for violating state law that prohibits sexual harassment and sex discrimination in promotions."[17] Furthermore, U.S. companies are hiring ethics officers "to develop ethics policies, listen to employees' complaints, conduct training, and investigate abuses such as sexual harassment."[18]

Different Standards

In "A Study of Occupational Departure of Employees in the Natural Sciences and Engineering," Anne Preston found only isolated instances of

---

[16] Marion Yuen, director of advisory services at Catalyst, presentation at the CWSE conference, Irvine, CA, January 17, 1993.

[17] Kevin G. Salwen, Labor letter: A special news report on people and their jobs in offices, fields, and factories, *The Wall Street Journal,* July 20, 1993.

[18] Julie Pomparano Lopez, Managing, *The Wall Street Journal,* May 10, 1993.

24

overt sexual harassment and sexual discrimination among the 50 women whom she interviewed. However, a common theme among all the women interviewed was their belief that they had to work harder than men to prove themselves. Many women felt they were judged by an entirely different set of standards and that respect came slowly at best.[19]

At the conference, women agreed that female managers tend to be interrupted more frequently than men and that their recommendations are ignored more frequently.[20] One woman felt that, from the beginning of her career, she had to build a reputation so superior that men were ill advised not to listen. After building this reputation, she felt she could never make a mistake. She went on to become senior vice-president of marketing in a major oil company, but she believes that she worked much harder than her male counterparts to get to that position. Corporate policies can work to change cultural habits that negatively affect women, but they cannot *quickly* undo long-term and deeply embedded cultural norms. Some of those policies to redress the effects of past policies are described in the next chapter of this report.

Both men and women at the CWSE conference said that men are often quick to challenge the findings of their female colleagues; it was also pointed out that women may be more sensitive to challenges by their

---

[19] Anne Preston, "A Study of Occupational Departure of Employees in the Natural Sciences and Engineering," presentation at the CWSE conference, Irvine, CA, January 17, 1993.

[20] Deborah Celentano Gerber was the first speaker at the CWSE conference to present this information, based on a survey she conducted with a number of women graduates of the Cornell University School of Engineering. However, it seems to be a pervasive experience of women scientists and engineers. Members of Systers, an electronic network, engaged in a lengthy discussion of their experiences, confirming conference findings, in May and June 1993. Such interruptions seem to follow a pattern established as early as elementary school. See, for instance, Jane Butler Kahle and Marsha Lakes Matyas, "Equitable Science and Mathematics Education: A Discrepancy Model," in Linda Skidmore Dix (ed.), *WOMEN: Their Underrepresentation and Career Differentials in Science and Engineering (Proceedings of a Workshop)*, Washington, DC: National Academy Press, 1987.

colleagues than are men. According to Preston, many of the women in her study had been proving themselves since high school, but the different standards on which they were judged only became evident during graduate school or when they entered the workplace. Few of those surveyed, however, exited a technological field because of double standards alone. The uphill battle for acceptance had become a way of life, despite its mental and emotional toll.

Similarly, in the Catalyst study, women who had been quite enthusiastic about the nature of their technological work during the training and early career stages were disappointed after choosing what they considered to be the path of more rapid advancement——management. In fact, they had chosen the more difficult path: women in the Catalyst study said that as managers they must continue to prove themselves, that their reputations are not as portable as those of their male peers, and that it was more difficult for them than for men to recover from management errors.

Conference participants tended to concur with the findings of these studies, believing that women scientists and engineers are often held to higher standards than men. This was felt to be true even for owners or chief executive officers of companies.

Styles of Communication

Some women pointed out that misunderstandings between men and women can occur in the workplace because of the different ways that men and women sometimes communicate and provide feedback. For example, when a manager says "no objection," a man often interprets the phrase to mean that he has the approval to proceed. A woman, by contrast, may interpret the phrase to mean the boss has no positive feelings about the issue: he is neither enthusiastic nor supportive, and therefore she should not proceed.[21]

---

[21] Rae Ann Hallstrom, presentation at the CWSE conference, Irvine, CA, January 17, 1993. See also, Norma Peterson, How do women manage?, *Executive Female* 7(4):45, July/August 1984; and Carol Berry, How to have clout at work and not talk like a man," *Savvy*, February 1986, p. 20.

26

Recent research in psychology and sociology has demonstrated that professional women tend to get person-centered feedback from their environment while professional men tend to get task-centered feedback.

Task-centered feedback consists of any response and commentary in a professional setting that is specific to the substance of the work done. . . . The commentator does not just compliment (or criticize) the performer generally or on his or her overall likability and "talent." (This would be "person-centered feedback.") Rather, the feedback (even when it is negative) continues the discussion in the direction that the presenter's work suggests. Thus, the performer can be truly flattered that the responder listened (observed, or read) closely, was instructed by the presenter's work, and has been stimulated to want to learn more.[22]

This phenomenon may be part of a systemic problem wherein males are not accustomed to seeing females as a source of information.

Perceptions of the Role of Women

An interesting dilemma has arisen in recent years as the work force has become diversified ethnically. Many ethnic groups have specific, sometimes limiting, perceptions of the roles of women; and, as female members of these groups are recruited more aggressively, those learned roles may prevent women, particularly minority women, from advancing in the industrial work force. For women from cultural groups that see them only as homemakers or in other "traditional female" occupations, there is a need to alter corporate cultures so that the values of nontraditional groups do not preclude contributions of women from those groups. One Hispanic scientist attending the CWSE conference noted that, in her family,

A woman's education was not as highly valued as a man's because men are supposed to be the breadwinners. Girls are raised with a different perspective and different role

---

[22] Sheila Tobias, a researcher who has contrasted the educational experiences of women and men, comments during the session on women in management, CWSE conference, Irvine, CA, January 17, 1993.

models than boys, and the culture expects them to fill those distinctive gender roles.

Cultural differences can have profound effects on one's career advancement. Conference participants cited research and their own experiences to note that women in certain cultures are not encouraged to speak up or to express opinions. For instance, an Asian American mechanical engineer noted, "Being a bachelor of science and Asian, I always yield to those who are wiser, those who are older than I. That's the way I've been taught all my years."

In contrast, Cynthia Martine, a Native American engineer, revealed that, because she came from a matrilineal tribe, she was taught to be a supporter of the family. She was never told she should not go to school; rather, her grandmother insisted that education was important to "survive in this white man's world." She was also taught to say what was on her mind. As a result, she feels that her cultural background has contributed to her advancement at a major U.S. company.

We conclude that the male culture is a source of difficulty for women scientists and engineers working in industry. However, genuine as are the problems discussed in this chapter, it should be acknowledged that many women tend to defeat themselves by low estimates of their abilities, low self-confidence, and low aspirations.

Retention

A critical factor that contributes to the underrepresentation of women scientists and engineers in industry, and which also has substantial financial implications for corporations, is the high attrition rate of women in S&E fields. In general, the exit rate of women in S&E jobs is considerably higher than men's; however, the exit rates for those in industry are even more dramatic, as noted in Chapter I. Moreover, women scientists and engineers in industrial jobs are both more likely to leave technical occupations and more likely to leave the labor force altogether than women employed in other sectors.

In this section we review additional data on retention[23] for women

---

[23] Among the studies that provided data on retention for the conference were those conducted by Anne Preston and Nancy DiTomaso. Some of the

and then discuss underlying causes of the high attrition. These include many of the problems identified in the previous section——that is, negative factors that characterize the workplace environment for women scientists and engineers in industry. Additional factors, presented in this section, are limited opportunities for career advancement, salary inequities, and work-family issues.

The analysis of the exit rate of S&E women from industry referred to in Chapter I also attempted to document the effects of observed variables on exit behavior, in particular the effects of age, field, occupation, and family characteristics. The result was that in multivariate models of exit behavior——even controlling for all these characteristics and comparing men and women with similar characteristics——women had more than twice the exit rate of men. Using these same multivariate models, the difference between the exit rate of women in industry and the exit rate of women in other sectors persisted. Figure II-1 shows the results from the multivariate model in which the ratio of exit rates is estimated. Women in industry were 30 percent more likely than women in other sectors to exit S&E jobs for other types of employment. They were about 80 percent more likely than women in government or the nonprofit sector to exit S&E jobs and actually become unemployed. Finally, women in industry were about 50 percent more likely than women in public or nonprofit jobs to exit the labor force entirely.

The Preston study revealed that men employed in private industry are 2.1 times as likely as men employed in the other sectors to leave science and engineering because of a promotion. Compared to men in the other two sectors, male scientists and engineers in private industry are 10 percent more likely to become employed outside science and engineering for reasons other than promotion, 2.4 times more likely to become unemployed, and 31 percent less likely to leave the labor force. In the areas of exit from science and engineering due to a promotion and due to unemployment, the sectoral exit

---

results of Anne Preston's study were presented in Chapter I. DiTomaso and her colleagues, with support from the Industrial Research Institute and the Center for Innovation Management Technology at Lehigh University, have studied the career experiences of women in industrial research and development (Nancy DiTomaso, George F. Farris, and Rene Cordero, "Women Scientists and Engineers: Gender Differences and a Model of Self-Assessment," presentation at the CWSE conference, Irvine, CA, January 17, 1993).

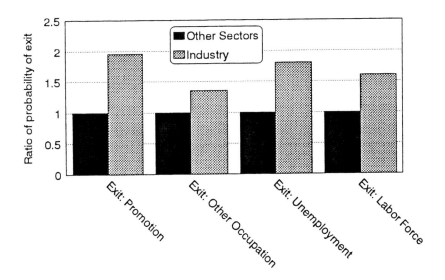

SOURCE: Anne Preston, "A Study of Occupational Departure of Employees in the Natural Sciences and Engineering," CWSE conference, Irvine, CA, January 17, 1993.

Figure II-1. Comparisons of the probabilities of exit of women in industry and women in other sectors, 1982-1989, by type of exit.

patterns are similar for men and women. However, women in industry are more likely to exit the labor force than women in other sectors, while men in industry are less likely to leave the labor force than are men in other sectors.

Two other findings from the study of National Science Foundation (NSF) data, for the period 1982-1989, are important. One is that exit rates were highest in the first 10 years. Beyond 10 years the exit rates of men and women begin to converge. Second, the study showed that family status, such as marriage or having children, had important effects on exit rates for both men and women, but the difference in exit rates of women across family status categories was small compared to the difference in exit rates between men and women within family status categories. Single women were much more likely to exit science and engineering than were single men. Married women without children were much more likely to

30

exit than married men without children, and women with children were much more likely to exit than were men with children.

A specific example discussed at the conference provides some insight. A high-tech company in Silicon Valley requested consultation due to the fact that very few senior women in the company could be retained. The pattern had been repeated over the past 5-10 years: there had been a nearly 100 percent turnover of this group of women. Two consultants met with several senior vice-presidents who were concerned about the problem as well as with senior women in the company. The women described, based on exit interviews and continuing social relationships with past female employees, how uncomfortable they had felt when they worked for the company. The senior vice-presidents believed that, when the company hired people, they were selected for excellence. However, they also made it clear that 90-95 percent of new technical employees were white men from a small number of elite universities. In the estimation of the consultants, the men from these schools formed an elitist corporate culture that excluded women's views. Therefore, it was not surprising to the consultants that women working in the company would find the environment hostile and not at all friendly to them. The senior vice-presidents failed to recognize that their views about who it was appropriate to hire were, in effect, blocking women from staying in the company, getting significant promotions, and rising to the top.[24]

The statistical studies and personal experiences presented at the conference documented many significant patterns and explained a great deal about exit behavior. It is important now to consider some of the underlying causes of this exit behavior.

Opportunities for Advancement

The reigning model for women entering S&E fields has been the pipeline model, which predicts that if more women enter the education and training end of the pipeline, the result will be more women emptying into the career field and progressing up the career ladder. The problem with the pipeline metaphor is that it is passive. Presumably, women enter the pipeline during the educational process, and, if they persevere, will have

---

[24] Myra H. Strober and Jay M. Jackman, "A Glassbreakers' Guide to the Ceiling," presentation at the CWSE conference, Irvine, CA, January 17, 1993.

opportunities to advance, like any male employee. The pipeline metaphor, however, does not take account of the possibility that the pipeline itself and the "pond" into which it empties may not be neutral.

In industry it is difficult to disprove the pipeline theory because a typical career path from entry to senior executive may take 20-25 years and there have not yet been sufficient numbers of women at the various levels to test the model. However, medicine may offer an instructive example: women have been in medicine in large numbers for the past 20 years, yet the number of women who are chairs of departments in medical schools across the United States virtually has not changed,[25] and in 1992, only one U.S. medical school was headed by a female dean, Nancy Gary at the Defense Department's Uniformed Services University of the Health Sciences.[26] Similarly, in investment banking and accounting, where an employee can move from entry level to partner in 10-12 years, women have not advanced to the extent expected. According to Strober,[27]

> Enough women entered those fields 10-12 years ago that,
> if the pipeline theory were working, a much higher
> percentage of partners would be women than is the case
> today.

Barriers to women in management can be subtle or overt. It is no secret that

hiring and promotion practices have kept top management

---

[25] Women in Medical Services Office, *Women in Medicine in America: In the Mainstream*, Chicago: American Medical Association, 1991.

[26] Constance Holden (ed.), One-of-a-kind dean, *Science* **256**(5058): 740, May 8, 1992.

[27] See Lean Nathans Spiro, The angry voices at Kidder, *Business Week,* February 1, 1993, pp. 60-63; Ceil Moran Pillsbury, Liza Capozzoli, and Amy Ciampa, A synthesis of research studies regarding the upward mobility of women in public accounting, *Accounting Horizons,* March 1989, pp. 63-70; and Brenda M. Hudson, Getting to the top: Upward mobility of women in the profession, *Pennsylvania CPA Journal,* Winter 1991, pp. 26-29.

jobs overwhelmingly for white males for a quarter of a century after the Civil Rights Act guaranteed equal employment opportunities for women and minorities. Preliminary results from a new study by Korn Ferry show that 95% of the top executive jobs are held by white males.[28]

Some corporate leaders are aware that the talent pool of women, particularly minority women, in science and engineering has largely been underutilized, although this pool offers potential managerial expertise. For instance, as DuPont executives have pointed out:[29]

Companies which are doing well in providing upward mobility are the ones that have been willing [to promote] women and minorities to the upper echelons. They have found that with proper preparation, these people are coming through for them. . . .[30]

There is a great satisfaction when an employee in a really demanding job comes through for you. This is especially true for women and minorities because they are newer to management ranks. Each time that happens, the management gains added confidence in giving the next person a chance at a demanding assignment.[31]

The formal presentations and discussions at the CWSE conference revealed a variety of business and personal reasons for women scientists

---

[28] Betty M. Vetter, *Scientific and Engineering Manpower Comments*, **27**(8), October 1990.

[29] DuPont, *op. cit.*

[30] Stacey J. Mobley, vice president of external affairs at E. I. dupont de Nemours and Company, in DuPont, *op. cit.*

[31] C. L. "Terry" Henry, group vice president for electronics at E. I. dupont de Nemours and Company, in DuPont, *op. cit.*

and engineers to pursue a management career. U.S. companies are coming to realize that "diversity of talent, experience, and perspective is good for business," according to Barbara Link, manager of application engineering at General Electric Corporation. At the same time, women have many personal reasons for moving from the technical to the management career ladder, including:

- the ability to have a larger impact on the company's success;
- the opportunity to use their communication and interpersonal skills in a people-focused, as well as a product-focused, situation;
- challenges to use a variety of skills, in areas such as leadership, budget and money management, and technology; and
- greater opportunities for advancement, recognition, and rewards.

One way to advance in industry is by moving laterally. Other conference participants agreed with Cynthia Martine, a Native American engineer employed at Eastman Kodak Company: "It is to your advantage to move around [in a company] so that you can gain experience from all sides of the business." However, lateral moves may be perceived by women as risky, particularly since women's reputations are often not as portable as men's.[32] According to a microbiologist attending the CWSE conference, promotion was almost always bestowed on those who had taken lateral transfers, but some women do not seem to be comfortable with that strategy.

Certainly there are no hard and fast rules on how to succeed in management; one vice-president of engineering said at the conference:

> I have a continually evolving view of what it takes to move
> up the management chain in industry and how to change
> the environment along the way. What has impressed me
> recently is that the rules, or maybe the emphasis on the
> rules, change quite a bit as one moves up the management
> ladder.[33]

---

[32] See, for instance, Joann S. Lublin, Strategic sidling: Lateral moves aren't always a mistake, *The Wall Street Journal*, August 4, 1993.

[33] Jill Wittels, vice president of engineering at Loral Infrared & Imaging

However, both women and men sometimes have difficulties in companies because they fail to understand what is required for promotion. Women tend to believe that if they work hard and do a fine job, they will be rewarded. Conference participants described personal experiences showing that rewards often do not result from such effort. Instead, many conferees emphasized the importance of becoming visible to upper management, to let them know what you have accomplished and that you are ready for promotion. While men also may find it difficult to do this, it may be more difficult for some women, those who are less assertive.

In some of the companies studied by Catalyst, the top levels of management had indeed been drawn from engineering ranks. In general, however, the highest level that most female engineers reached was the third or the fourth level beyond entry level. Interestingly, even in companies where there were women in top management positions, some female engineers still felt they were stuck at the third or fourth level beyond entry level.[34]

Preliminary findings from a Families and Work Institute (FWI) study, "Barriers and Opportunities for Women Scientists and Engineers in the Pharmaceutical and Automotive Industries," revealed some interesting disparities between men's and women's views about career opportunities and also a paradox that may say something disturbing about women's expectations. When women and men were asked "Does your company do a good job of developing employees?," neither women nor men gave their companies very high marks (Figure II-2). However, men's confidence in career development increased as they moved from early- to mid-career, presumably because of their own rewarding career experiences. In contrast, many women who started off quite sanguine about career opportunities had become disillusioned by mid-career.

Arlene Johnson, vice-president of FWI, found it interesting to compare these findings to responses to the statement "My supervisor values my work." In the three age groups of the FWI study,[35] men consistently

---

Systems, speaking at the CWSE conference, Irvine, CA, January 17, 1993.

[34] Marion Yuen, *op. cit.*

[35] Group I=ages 22-30, Group II=ages 31-44, and Group III=ages 45 + .

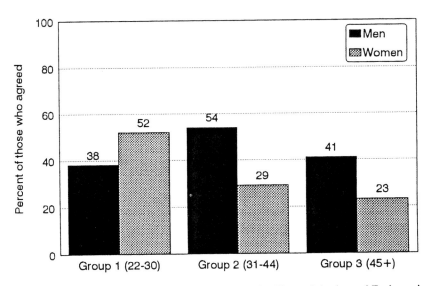

SOURCE: Arlene Johnson, "Barriers and Opportunities for Women Scientists and Engineers in the Pharmaceutical and Automotive Industries," CWSE conference, Irvine, CA, January 17, 1993.

Figure II-2. Response to the statement, "The company does a good job developing employees."

perceived their work to be valued while women consistently believed their work to be undervalued.

> What is suggested is that younger women may be preoccupied with the impression they create, but they have confidence in the system, whereas older or mid-career women feel more confident in their skills and how they are being valued in their own work group, but many have lost confidence that the system will work for them.[36]

---

[36] Arlene Johnson, "Barriers and Opportunities for Women Scientists and Engineers in the Pharmaceutical and Automotive Industries," CWSE conference, Irvine, CA, January 17, 1993.

Not surprisingly, when women and men were asked whether women have the same opportunities for advancement, they disagreed. Most men believed there was equal opportunity, and this finding was fairly constant across the three age groups. Women's skepticism about equal opportunity, however, became more hardened with their years of experience.[37]

There is, however, a paradox. When asked "Is this a good company for women and minorities?," women in the FWI study——with the exception of the late-career group——were quite complimentary toward their companies. Of the mid-career group of women, only 20 percent thought they had equal opportunity, but 68 percent said the company was a good one for women and minorities. Ms. Johnson's speculation about this paradox was:

First, each of these companies had recently promulgated some new policies and programs, either in recruitment and retention or in the work and family areas. Perhaps these companies were getting a great deal of credit for announcing the programs, even though the effects of the programs had not yet been felt. Second, what might also be suggested is that the doors are, in fact, closed——that is, women do not have equal opportunity, but neither do they expect it, and in the end, they feel they will not do better elsewhere.

The latter explanation is disturbing. It suggests that women in corporations are not capable of creating change, and that there will be no groundswell in these companies. If women continue to perceive that their companies are not as bad as others and that situations really cannot get any better, then they have no motivation for taking the risks necessary to advocate for change.[38]

---

[37] *Ibid.*

[38] *Ibid.*

Salary Discrepancies

Another important factor contributing to the high attrition of women from S&E employment is inequitable salary treatment:

Average annual salaries of women scientists and engineers are lower than those of men. This difference may stem at least in part from differences in degree fields, degree levels, experience levels, employment sectors, labor market behavior, or a combination of these variables.[39]

In its latest report detailing salaries for scientists and engineers, NSF reports:

In 1986, the average annual salaries of women scientists and engineers were about 75 percent of men's salaries. In 1990, the median annual salary for women who had received S&E bachelor's degrees in 1988 or 1989 was $21,000, about 73 percent of the $29,500 median salary of men. For recent master's S&E degree recipients in 1990 (degree granted in 1988 or 1989), the ratio was 84 percent ($32,800 for women versus $39,000 for men). In 1989, among Ph.D.'s with one year or less of professional experience, the median salary for women ($35,500) was 88 percent of the median salary for men ($40,400).

In comparison, ratios of women's salaries to men's in the overall work force in 1990 (based on median weekly earnings) were 73 percent for all full-time wage and salary workers over age 25, 74 percent for full-time wage and salary workers in professional occupations, and 89 percent for full-time wage and salary engineers. [These differences were] partially due to the relatively low salaries earned by individuals in psychology, the life sciences, and the social sciences. In the computer specialties——the fastest growing

---

[39] Patricia E. White (ed.), *Women and Minorities in Science and Engineering: An Update* (NSF 92-303), Washington, DC: National Science Foundation, 1992.

38

field for both women and men during the eighties——
women's salaries averaged about 85 percent of those for
men. For engineers, the salary ratio was 83 percent, with
some fluctuations among major engineering fields.

Women doctoral scientists with one year or less of
professional experience earned 96 percent of what men
earned ($35,200 versus $36,700) and engineers 98 percent
($47,700 versus $48,500). By field, the ratio for doctoral
scientists ranged from 89 percent (environmental sciences)
to 104 percent (psychology).[40]

Although women may experience higher starting salaries than men,[41]
eventually the salaries of men exceed those of women who have attained the
same degree level and years of experience.

Scant literature exists on racial differences in earnings among
females, by S&E subfield. However, NSF reports:

Salary discrepancies exist not only between men
and women, but between women of different races. Whites
earned the highest average annual salaries among women
scientists and engineers. In 1986, white women scientists
earned an average of $29,400, compared with $28,800 for
Asian[42] women scientists and $25,400 for black women

---

[40] *Ibid.*

[41] In 1990 the differences in median salaries of recent graduates (those
earning their degrees in 1988 and 1989), based on gender, continued:
women holding bachelor's degrees in S&E disciplines earned salaries larger
than those of their male counterparts, on average, in only chemical,
mechanical, and petroleum engineering; at the master's level, the average
salaries of women exceeded those of men only in the social sciences and in
civil, industrial, and materials engineering [National Science Board, *Science
& Engineering Indicators: 1991* (NSB 91-1), Washington, DC: National
Science Foundation, Appendix Tables 3-5 and 3-6].

[42] It should be noted here that, although NSF and other data-collecting
agencies report information for Asians collectively, each subgroup of Asians

scientists. Among engineers, Asian women earned the highest annual salary——an average of $35,000 in 1986. Comparable salaries for white women engineers and black women engineers were $34,300 and $32,900, respectively. At the doctoral level in 1989, Asian women again had the highest median salaries——$45,800 compared with $44,700 for white women, $44,400 for black women, and $43,500 for Native American women.

Regardless of racial group, women scientists and engineers reported median annual salaries lower than those of men of the same race. The differential between the salaries of Asian women and Asian men was the largest. In 1986, Asian women earned salaries equal to 74 percent of Asian men's salaries, black women's median salaries were equal to 78 percent of black men's salaries, and white women's salaries were equal to 76 percent of white men's salaries. Among doctoral scientists, the differences between women's and men's salaries were not as large. In 1989, at the doctoral level, black women's salaries were 87 percent of black men's salaries, Asian women's salaries were 82 percent of Asian men's, and white women's were 79 percent of white men's.[43]

Research has shown that many minority women experience discrimination based on both sex and ethnicity——for instance, minority women have more difficulty accessing higher-paying occupations than do Caucasian women, even after controlling for such factors as schooling and work.

Work-Family Issues

According to Jacqueline M. Akinpelu, head of the Network Capacity Operation Systems Planning Department, AT&T Bell Laboratories,

---

(e.g., Pacific Islanders, Filipinos, Koreans) has a different participation rate within science and engineering, and all subgroups should not be treated as a single group.

[43] *Ibid.*

Balance between career and personal life will almost always become a critical issue. In order to handle it effectively, you must always retain responsibility for managing your own expectations and defining your success. This is especially difficult for the woman highly motivated by achievement and recognition on the job.[44]

Women and men who choose to both practice science and engineering and have families must face reality: it *is* difficult to achieve both career and family success. A male scientist reported to the Committee on Women in Science and Engineering:

Men, for whatever reason, generally put job ahead of family. The results are often disastrous on the family front and men regret that they did not do more with their family, both wife and children. But all this says, nevertheless, is that most people cannot excel at both. This is true for men as well as for women.

Thus, addressing work-family issues is essential if companies are to achieve high retention of their employees, both women and men, who have family responsibilities. As is reported in all employment sectors, conference participants cited family issues, particularly motherhood, as a major reason that in industry women are not promoted as often as men. One conference presenter defined "a mother's dilemma":

how to continue working at the exciting career she's trained for while also wanting and/or needing to spend time with her children, whether they are toddlers or teenagers, without being drop-kicked out of the race to advance and into the dead-end career zone at work.[45]

Other conference participants agreed that, once a woman becomes a mother,

---

[44] Jacqueline Akinpelu, presentation at the CWSE conference, Irvine, CA, January 17, 1993.

[45] Rae Ann Hallstrom, *op. cit.*

it is nearly impossible to avoid being treated differently. This is especially true if she experiences her pregnancy while on the job. Following her return to work, frequently she is given assignments that are less desirable, those that involve limited travel, and those that involve less physical risk.

To prevent negative career effects, many women are careful to time their pregnancies. One conference participant described her strategy this way, and others agreed that it was a good approach:

> I think it is possible to have a family in this company, but
> you have to time it. Wait until you get the promotion, but
> then don't have the children too late. You have to be
> careful not to advance so far, and then get knocked out of
> consideration because of having children.

This confirms findings of a recent international study by Francine Blau and Lawrence Kahn, economists at the University of Illinois, Urbana-Champaign:

> Only the United States fails to guarantee the right to
> maternity leave beyond the period of actual disability.
> Indeed, most other countries guarantee time off with pay for
> both pregnancy and care for infants. It thus seems likely
> that more American women are forced to choose between
> high-paying careers and motherhood.[46]

Negative career effects can extend to women who are not married and not pregnant. Women at one company spoke of interviewing for positions within the company and being asked, "Are you married?" or "Are you going to have children?" These are illegal questions, but they are being asked widely anyway. One woman reported that she was denied a promotion because she had children, and another woman in the same focus group hid her pregnancy for 7½ months because she was seeking a promotion.[47] Discrimination against pregnant women does continue, despite federal legislation. In fact,

---

[46] Peter Passell, Women's work: The pay paradox, *The New York Times,* March 25, 1992, p. C2.

[47] Arlene Johnson, *op. cit.*

[t]hough 64% of the pregnancy discrimination claimants [in a 5-year study] worked for employers with 50 or more employees and would have been protected under the Family and Medical Leave Act [effective August 5, 1993], the remaining 36% of the women worked for companies too small to be covered.[48]

Women are advocating change in pregnancy and parental leave policies. Even in companies where maternity leave can be negotiated, the long-term question for women often is how to manage the pressure of the job and the demands of family. The length of the workday in industry, contrary to popular belief, is not predictable. The hours——very often beyond 40 per week——and on-the-job demands lead to what some call an unofficial competition for whose face can be seen the longest in the workplace. The energy addressed to this topic in focus groups of women of all ages in the FWI study, "Barriers and Opportunities for Women Scientists and Engineers in the Pharmaceutical and Automotive Industries," suggests that this is the pivotal issue that differentiates men's and women's career stages:[49]

Work-family policies [of a company] did not appear to affect recruitment, but they became very important when deciding whether to stay in a job, especially for early careerists. When survey respondents were asked, "How important is the balancing of your personal life with work?," it became very important for mid-careerists. It was

---

[48] Sue Shellenberger, Work & family, *The Wall Street Journal*, May 19, 1993. In her June 11, 1993, column, Shellenberger reported, "The law . . . gives workers up to 12 weeks of unpaid, job-protected leave with health benefits each year to care for a new child, ailing relative or one's own illness. Under the rules, a qualifying illness is any physical or mental ailment involving an overnight hospital stay or a three-day absence from work combined with continuing treatment or supervision by a doctor or other health-care professional. Also covered is any chronic condition that requires continuing medical treatment and would incapacitate the person for more than three days if left untreated."

[49] *Ibid.*

also notably important to men, much more so perhaps than many companies recognize.

Women in all career stages agreed that one of the greatest influences on their career was managing maternity. Many women perceived that taking time off to have a child is detrimental to one's career, in part because becoming a mother is taken as a sign that a woman is not dedicated to her job. Younger men, in particular, concurred with this perception. As one woman in the FWI study put it, "They feel that your priorities change, so they redirect your career path so as not to invest in you for the long term." Another female FWI interviewee said, "We have three pregnant women now in our group, and they know they will not be promoted."[50]

An interesting control group, or comparison, would be single-parent males and single-parent females. This could help to separate parenthood effects on career from gender effects on career. Narrow age cohorts would also contribute to an understanding of these effects since younger people, both women and men, are more sensitive to this issue.

How a company addresses dependent care, whether for one's children or one's parents (often called "elder care"), can also affect its ability to retain women scientists and engineers. A recent study by DiTomaso *et al.*[51] revealed that women with dependents had much more difficulty with dependent care than men with dependents, with one exception. Women experienced less difficulty when their spouse traveled than men did. The study by DiTomaso *et al.* also found a high correlation between the highest performers in the workplace, both men and women, and those who have

---

[50] In that group, according to Arlene Johnson, there had been many pregnancies; employees said that no one had ever gotten a promotion in the 18-24 months that surrounded their pregnancies.

[51] Nancy DiTomaso, George F. Farris, and Rene Cordero, "Women Scientists and Engineers: Gender Differences and a Model of Self-Assessment," presentation at the CWSE conference, Irvine, CA, January 17, 1993.

preschool children, which suggests that this should be a bottom-line issue for companies.

Men and women in "A Study of Occupational Departure of Employees in the Natural Sciences and Engineering," conducted by Anne Preston, were asked how they divided household chores and child-care responsibilities. Respondents, both women and men, agreed that women are responsible for about two-thirds of the household chores and child-care responsibilities. Clearly then, how to balance family and career remains more of a female consideration. What is striking is that the men and women of the sample were at much the same stages of their careers, were almost the same age, and had similar experience levels.[52]

An examination of the employment status of men and women in that study reveals a big difference between how men and women deal with family issues. Fourteen percent of the women were working part-time; only 1 percent of the men were. Sixteen percent of the women were not working, and a majority of them were not working for family reasons. Only 4 percent of the men were not working, and none had left because of family reasons. Women often seek flexible working arrangements. In her study, Dr. Preston found that women who held bachelor's and master's degrees were, in general, trying to establish a scientific career in industry or government. However, the women who found jobs in private industry were often stymied by the inflexibility of their companies regarding child-care issues. In particular, these women talked about an inability to obtain part-time work and flexible scheduling. Many women mentioned companies that were inflexible about their taking time off for sick children.

It is seen by some that the issue is structural to employment rather than to gender. One male scientist reported to the Committee:

> Work [in industry] is viewed by the organization as central,
> and anything that interferes with it is discouraged, for both
> men and women equally. The driving force in work is that
> an organization must compete with others serving the same
> market.

However, as will be detailed in the next chapter, many large companies have

---

[52] Anne Preston, *op. cit.*

found it possible (possibly advantageous) to make available part time work and some flexibility in hours. In any case, Preston's research found that,

> when these barriers begin to influence negatively the women's lives, they often leave the labor force for a while. When they return to industrial employment, it is often difficult to return to science and engineering, which have progressed in their absence; they begin new occupations.[53]

To prevent the collision of family and job commitments, women long for more flexibility. One FWI interviewee said,

> I enjoy working for this company, but there is no way that I will be able to devote as much time to work when I have a family. Work in this company has to be your number one priority. My management and all the people who have been successful have sacrificed their family and personal life.[54]

Corporate research shows that this pattern of unilateral dedication to the job and sacrificing of family interactions is found for both women and men.[55]

The principal problem that men and women in the FWI study reported about work-family programs was that the very companies that were touted for their "family-friendly" policies were often those where people were afraid to use the programs for fear of being penalized. Therefore, the key, as some said, is to "decriminalize" part-time work and to make job-sharing and part-time employment viable options for committed careerists.[56]

---

[53] *Ibid.*

[54] Arlene Johnson, *op. cit.*

[55] See, for instance, DuPont, *op. cit.*, and The Institute of Electrical and Electronics Engineers Inc., *IEEE Spectrum: Diversity at Work,* New York: IEEE, June 1992.

[56] Arlene Johnson, *op. cit.*

A third work-family issue is how companies accommodate dual-career couples. According to Preston, "Many Ph.D. women are looking to private industry as a solution, particularly with regard to dual-career problems."[57] They perceived industry as having more jobs, jobs that are more geographically dispersed, and jobs that do not require outside funding. Although these women saw industry as a solution, it was also a compromise. Moving to industry, as they perceived it coming out of graduate school, meant taking a less prestigious job.[58]

Many companies take pride in employing multiple members of the same family. However, several conference participants reported that other companies still will not hire two people from the same family. Certainly, few companies will hire two family members for the same department because it is considered, in general, poor management practice. As a result, many times, when one spouse gets an industrial job, the other must take a teaching job in a community college. It may be underutilization of the spouse, but at least it is a job, whereas there may be no chance for a second industrial job.

Furthermore, competitor-exclusion rules in companies also work against dual careers. For example, if a woman is working for pharmaceutical company A, pharmaceutical company B will not hire her husband because of the possibility of their sharing competitors' secrets. In that case she is unlikely to take the job in the first place because doing so might eliminate his chances for a job and therefore reduce the family income. A man can also not take the job because doing so might eliminate his wife's chance of a job, with similar results. However, this seems to occur less frequently.

Particularly in the pharmaceutical industry, there is the problem of geography. Most companies are situated on the East and West coasts. If one spouse gets a job with the only pharmaceutical company in a particular city, there often is no second company or related pharmaceutical job for the other spouse; Jane S. Allen, a toxicologist at GLAXO Inc., noted, however, that this company has "no rules forbidding employment of spouses." In engineering the situation is better; companies are more widely dispersed geographically.

Being a scientist or engineer in a dual-career marriage has profound

---

[57] Anne Preston, *op. cit.*

[58] *Ibid.*

47

effects and influences on both individuals, the marriage, and probably their companies as well. A computer scientist described her dual-career marriage——one that is without children but involves a parent who is partially handicapped——as difficult but workable and, in the long term, satisfying. She and her husband have similar technological backgrounds. They met in graduate school and actually worked and were recruited together because of the similarities in their training. From the start the couple decided to give their careers equal priority, a decision that is probably more common at the Ph.D. level. Although they both thought their first jobs would be in academe, in fact, the academic job offers were in parts of the country or at universities where equally challenging opportunities were not available for both of them. Consequently, they began their careers in industry, something they consider to be positive today because they have gained experience in areas they probably would not have chosen otherwise. The couple has been together for about 16 years and, according to the speaker, it took probably half of that time to work out a balance where they found it easy to be in the same field. Several factors made their dual-career marriage work. First, they developed personal identities and mutual respect. Second, when the couple worked in the same place, each was direct about his or her responsibilities, work schedules, and long-term plans. Mutual cooperation, communication, and compromise were absolutely necessary.

Balance between career and personal life will always be a stressful issue for women, perhaps more so for those in management because of their increased visibility and responsibility in the workplace. It is potentially as stressful for men, reported a male scientist. However, one female scientist at the conference felt that, in order to balance career and family issues effectively,

> [w]omen must retain responsibility for managing their own expectations and definitions of success. That is difficult to do in the corporate environment because there is a strong male-established definition of what it means to be successful.[59]

As regards the many corporate practices that make it more difficult for women to perform their jobs and to advance, we note that there is nothing

---

[59] Akinpelu, *op. cit*

inherently valid or invalid about the way companies or businesses are organized and operate; policies take on a life of their own, and because they exist, they appear to be valid.

A solution for this problem, according to Strober and Jackman, would be to provide feedback to all executives, who are often the defenders of these patterns and policies.[60] They could be informed of policies that undermine the capacity of women to function and to advance in the organization and of the losses to the company of employees who have the intelligence and skills to do the job but whose efforts and career paths have been hindered. As is discussed in the next chapter, considerable progress has already been made in this direction.

---

[60] Strober and Jackman, *op. cit.*

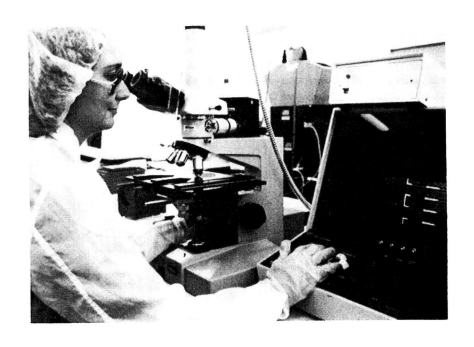

Sue Stuber, manager of the Large Area Silicon Array Prototyping Group at Xerox's Palo Alto Research Center, inspects silicon wafers for defects. (Photo: Xerox Corporation)

III. CORPORATE INITIATIVES
TO RECRUIT AND RETAIN WOMEN
SCIENTISTS AND ENGINEERS

Some companies have made great strides in developing programs—to a large extent, gender-independent—to recruit and retain their technological work forces. At the conference sponsored by the Committee on Women in Science and Engineering (CWSE), several efforts by six U.S. companies were presented as models of what is being done in this area as well as others targeting women scientists and engineers. It was pointed out throughout the conference that programs established initially to diversify the corporate work force generally have had positive effects on the recruitment and retention of both women and men in those companies. Another point reiterated during the presentations about effective programs was that the commitment of top management is essential for the successful implementation and longevity of the programs.

A Look at Six Companies

Xerox Corporation, ALCOA, Aerospace Corporation, AT&T Bell Laboratories, and Scios Nova illustrate what are, by current standards, programs that are effective in recruiting and ensuring the professional progress of women scientists and engineers in industry. Conference participants considered other companies, as well, to be model companies in their efforts to recruit and retain women in their technical work force. One such model of a small company, Barrios Technology, will be discussed as a further illustrative example.

Xerox Corporation[61]

Xerox Corporate Research and Technology (CR&T) is working deliberately toward making Xerox Corporation "the employer of choice for women and minorities by the year 2000," according to Marcia Bush,

---

[61] Drawn from presentations at the CWSE conference, Irvine, CA, January 17-18, 1993, by Marcia Bush, manager, Speech and Signal Processing Area, and Leslie Jill Miller, manager, Systems Sciences Laboratory, Xerox Corporation.

manager of Speech and Signal Processing at the Xerox Palo Alto Research Center. Xerox hopes to achieve a balanced work force that reflects the diversity and availability of technical personnel in the marketplace. It is focusing on increasing diversity within corporate research, principally for women, both at the individual-contributor level and in management.

How did such a goal come about? The motivation was primarily a business one. Demographic trends indicate that growth in the work force between now and the year 2000 will be primarily among women and minorities. In order to help position CR&T to attract the best scientists and engineers, a Women's Council was formed in 1991 to advise senior management on issues related to recruiting and retaining women. The Council was originally composed of nine representatives from Xerox's Corporate Research Centers; currently it consists of 13 representatives from the expanded CR&T organization.

Two-day meetings of the Council have been held every three months, with executive minutes distributed to senior managers within CR&T. The Council meets with women at the individual centers to obtain their input and also to provide them with feedback on Council activities. Recommendations by the Council are communicated by directed memos and directed presentations at meetings of senior CR&T staff. Presentations are also made at the Center level.

At its first meeting, the Council developed a mission statement:

> To advise CR&T management on how to achieve its vision of being the employer of choice for technical and technical support women. The CR&T Women's Council recognizes the value of diversity and envisions a work force within CR&T which exemplifies the diversity of our society. We are committed to substantially increased representation of both majority and minority women within CR&T and within CR&T management.[62]

At the same time, Council members identified five problem areas to be addressed by CR&T: increased numbers of women in corporate research (only 10 percent of the Ph.D.s in positions leading to senior management at Xerox are women), career development, salary equity, working

---

[62] Leslie Jill Miller, speaking at the CWSE conference, Irvine, CA, January 17, 1993.

environment, and benefits. Subsequently, the Council determined that salary equity was not a problem. It then prepared recommendations for improving the hiring and promotion of women scientists and engineers that include the following:

- establish an outward focus with greater emphasis on fellowship programs—that is, financial aid to female graduate students and, potentially, internships with the company—and the recruitment of women,
- create internal hiring opportunities that would promote cross-organizational flow (i.e., movement from one area of the company to another, often associated with lateral transfers),
- clarify the criteria to be met by a person seeking a promotion, and
- publicize internal job opportunities throughout the company.

Because the Council is concerned with establishing linkages with universities, it is revising the Xerox fellowship programs to make them more effective and to establish more contact between graduate students supported by Xerox and researchers at the research laboratories.

Increasing the flow within the organization and into the business units of Xerox is important for creating hiring opportunities when the labs are not increasing in size. The Council has also recommended examination of cross-laboratory promotion statistics to identify any discrepancies between men and women or across the labs in different geographical locations.

In addition to hiring and promotion recommendations to Xerox CR&T management, the Women's Council has developed a set of career and development recommendations for individual employees and managers. Women scientists and engineers are encouraged to set objectives, meet performance requirements, know their organization, and seek development opportunities. At the same time, recommendations to technical managers center on three broad actions: communicate, proactively support career planning, and set up and actively support career development opportunities. These recommendations are summarized in Appendix B.[63]

---

[63] Meritocracy is a worthwhile goal of all employers. However, it should be noted that in some companies career advancement does not always result from one's achievements.

The Council has also been involved in another important entity at Xerox, the Women Managers Roundtable, which is charged with "making issues visible to corporate management." At the annual meeting of the Roundtable, representatives from major Xerox organizations meet with Xerox's chief executive officer (CEO) and corporate human resources staff to discuss the concerns of women at Xerox. The 1992 meeting focused on three main issues: management behavior and culture, representation of women in the company's work force, and career development. Representatives pointed out both negative and positive achievements of the preceding year. For instance, Xerox had undergone a major reorganization and had made many new appointments, several of which had gone to women. However, while everyone agreed that the very top management at Xerox is committed to women's issues, this commitment has not yet filtered down through other levels of management. Roundtable representatives felt it was incumbent upon the CEO to start changing the culture, to continue to be a mentor, and to actively communicate his attitudes to lower levels of the organization.

Initially, all members of the Council were at the management level or its equivalent in the scientific track and paid for travel and hotel expenses out of their group budgets. Recently, there has been a move toward more centralized funding (e.g., from research laboratory budgets), in order to facilitate the Council's goal of including women at lower grade levels in its membership and to stress the importance of the Council's work to those larger entities. Meals and other on-site meeting expenses continue to be covered at the CR&T organizational level.

ALCOA[64]

ALCOA Technical Center (ATC), the central research facility of the Aluminum Company of America (ALCOA), is a leader in the materials science industry and also a leader in developing programs for attracting and retaining talented women and minorities in its work force. Since 1990, ATC has developed several effective policies and programs to help employees balance work and family responsibilities, according to Ophelia

---

[64] Drawn from the presentation by Ophelia R. Scott, staff administrator, Human Resources and Industrial Relations Department, ALCOA Technical Center, during the CWSE conference, Irvine, CA, January 18, 1993.

Scott, staff administrator for the Department of Human Resources and Industrial Relations.

In the late 1980s, staffing levels at ALCOA Technical Center were on the rise, and the center was interested in hiring to enhance the diversity of its work force. However, it became apparent to ATC management that traditional recruitment methods were not producing advanced degree minority and female scientists and engineers interested in long-term research. Therefore, ATC representatives traveled to historically black colleges and universities and other universities with a substantial minority enrollment to learn how to recruit and how to develop effective university relations on these campuses.

ALCOA Technical Center then developed and implemented the Pilot School Program to increase ATC's presence on selected college campuses, to identify talented undergraduate female and minority S&E students, and to create technical linkages with the pilot schools. Selection of the pilot schools was based on the quality of technical programs, size of the minority population, and number of female and minority students who obtained advanced degrees. In one instance, proximity to ALCOA Technical Center also was a factor. The Pilot School Program is not a human resources program. Each university in the program is assigned an ATC coordinator—a scientist or engineer who ensures division involvement and establishes technology linkages vital to the Center's long-term relationship with that university. This involvement might include participation in career fairs; on-campus recruiting; formal or informal visits with students, faculty, and administrators; on-campus seminars, both technical and nontechnical; and the identification and funding of technical research of interest to ATC, with involvement of women and minority students. ALCOA Technical Center benefits from the Pilot School Program by the identification of students for its Summer Professional Employment Program, candidates for existing job openings, students to be tracked for future employment, and also candidates for fellowships. Since 1991, when the program became fully operational, 15 summer interns have been placed through the pilot school initiative, four of whom were female. Two permanent positions also have been filled through these efforts, one by a woman.

Through the awarding of fellowships and scholarships, corporations can develop relationships with high-potential female and minority candidates. At ALCOA, scholarships are awarded to undergraduate students at those universities in ALCOA Technical Center's Pilot School Program. Scholarship recipients are offered summer internships as part of

ATC's ongoing efforts to identify and develop a pool of candidates for future staffing needs. The scholarship program has several benefits, including the development of name recognition for ALCOA; the development of linkages with specific academic departments; and the initiation of relationships with particular students.

In ALCOA's Minority Fellowship Program, which is fairly recent in origin, a significant long-term relationship can be developed between the company and a future employee. The award process was developed and finalized in late 1992. In early 1993 there were four ALCOA Technical Center fellows; two were women. They are nominated by, and must have a financial commitment from, a research division. Candidates are selected for fellowships based on participation and performance in the summer intern program, interest in research, scholastic records, references, and compatibility with the ALCOA Technical Center. A fellowship review committee selects the candidates, and approval for a successful candidate is granted by ALCOA's executive vice-president of research and development and ATC's Operations Management Lead Team. Division commitment to the candidate is vital to the fellowship process and to the linkage between the fellow and ATC. Typically, a fellow chooses, with the assistance of the sponsoring research division, a thesis topic that furthers the ATC's own research interests. The division also assists the fellow in selecting a university for graduate study and provides discussion on potential career opportunities within ALCOA Technical Center. ALCOA's financial commitment to the fellow includes tuition, fees, books and supplies, a monthly stipend, and summer employment. Upon completion of the Ph.D., fellowship awardees enter into employment with ALCOA.

The ALCOA Technical Center's program on work-family issues will be detailed later in this chapter.

Aerospace Corporation[65]

At Aerospace Corporation in 1962, there were *12 women (.01 percent)* employees in technical positions; today women comprise *12.5 percent* (or 313 out of 2,507) of the technical work force. At

---

[65] Drawn from the presentation at the CWSE conference, Irvine, CA, January 18, 1993, by Shirley McCarty, general manager of human resources at Aerospace Corporation.

Aerospace, recruitment of women is aided by the involvement of many women in mentoring—a positive signal that attracts women to the company. The fact that senior women mentor men also signals that the company values women's work equally with men's. Aerospace policies and practices are attractive to women, and many dedicated people are working toward creating a positive climate that contributes to the successful recruitment of women. "Overall," according to Shirley McCarty, "the human resources policies at Aerospace are gender blind and ethnically blind."

Women's committees or networks within a company can be vitally important influences on the recruitment and retention of women. The Women's Committee at Aerospace has been not only a leader for change, but also a strong support system that has helped women gain confidence. An active organization since 1973 with membership throughout the company—including secretarial staff, technical staff, and management—the committee has met annually with the president and has been involved in numerous issues, including:

- the development of a maternity leave policy;
- equalization of employee benefits for secretarial and technical staff;
- establishing awards for women; and
- researching and making recommendations to the president and executive staff on female candidates for the Board of Directors, thereby creating female role models for women in the company.

Further details on the work-family aspects of the Aerospace program are given later in the chapter.

AT&T Bell Laboratories[66]

Naomi Behrman noted that managers at AT&T Bell Laboratories "value both women and men employees who are well grounded in their technical expertise and who have an understanding of the business world." She stated that AT&T Bell Laboratories is committed to encouraging this

---

[66] Drawn from the presentation by Naomi Behrman, coordinator of employee counseling services, AT&T Bell Laboratories Health Services Group, at the CWSE conference, Irvine, CA, January 17, 1993.

broader base of knowledge and improving the working climate for its female employees.

AT&T Bell Laboratories has developed, collaboratively with human resources and technical staff, a University Relations Summer Program similar to the one at ALCOA. It provides work experience in an R&D environment for "outstanding B.S., M.S., and Ph.D. minority students" in 12 fields of science and engineering: chemistry, computer science/ engineering, electrical engineering, mechanical engineering, operations research, chemical engineering, physics, mathematics, information science, communication science, statistics, and materials science. The Summer Research Program is similar but focuses on the identification and nurturing of research ability in women and minorities, thus increasing their representation in science and engineering (S&E) careers.

AT&T Bell Laboratories also offers both scholarships and fellowships to talented students in science and engineering. The Engineering Scholarship Program "is designed to increase the talent pool by providing financial assistance to outstanding underrepresented minorities and women high school seniors who have been admitted to full-time studies" in computer science/engineering, electrical engineering, mechanical engineering, or systems engineering. The Cooperative Research Fellowship Program (CRFP) encourages the development of scientific and research ability in underrepresented minorities by establishing successful mentor and student relationships, promoting student participation in an active industrial research environment, and providing financial support. AT&T Bell Laboratories' Graduate Research Program for Women has goals similar to those of CRFP. Begun in 1975, the program awards both fellowships and grants (Table III-1). Fellowships provide an annual stipend for tuition and fees, textbooks and living allowance, summer employment, reimbursement for travel to scientific conferences, and an AT&T Bell Laboratories' scientist as a mentor. Grants provide a smaller amount annually, to be used by the recipient in any way that benefits her professional development. Grant recipients can also be eligible for summer employment and are also assigned an AT&T Bell Laboratories' scientist as a mentor.

Another recent effort at AT&T is sponsorship (with the National Science Foundation and other U.S. companies) of the Women in Engineering Program Advocates Network. The program began at three institutions—Stevens Institute of Technology, Purdue University, and the University of Washington in Seattle—"because of their positive records of

TABLE III-1: Summary Data, AT&T Bell Laboratories' Graduate
Research Program for Women, 1975-1992

Type of Award	Fellowships	Grants	Combination: Fellows/Grants
Graduates	23	33	
Discipline			
Physics		21	
Chemistry			11
Computer science			6
Mathematics			5
Materials science			4
Electrical engineering			3
Operations research			3
Other		3	
Employment sector			
Industry	9	13	
Hired by AT&T Bell Laboratories	4	4	
Academe	7	8	
Postdoc	5	9	
Unknown	2	3	
Withdrawals	10	10	
Still in program	18	41	
TOTAL participants	51	84	

SOURCE: Naomi Behrman, presentation at the CWSE conference, Irvine, CA, January 17, 1993.

working with women."[67] Women in Engineering programs at those three institutions include efforts to increase the numbers of women studying engineering, establishing mentoring and summer internships involving the private sector, and finding positions for women engineering graduates. Particularly noteworthy is that WEPAN continues to work with women even after they are in their first corporate positions.

Available to all employees at AT&T Bell Laboratories, the Employee Counseling Service is a highly effective program that has been offered since 1977. It provides private and confidential one-on-one counseling sessions, consults with management about special organizational and individual issues, and affects the environment of whole organizations by presenting special seminars and workshops on subjects such as balancing work and family, single working parents, and dual-career couples. Details of AT&T Bell Laboratories' work-family programs are given later in the chapter.

Specific topics arising out of the work problems of managers and employees are also addressed for specific organizations. Problems can become overwhelming when there is a combination of pressures—for example, a job change, a relocation, and a family unit affected by all of these changes. Individuals can usually handle the stress of any one of these situations in isolation, but when pressured on several fronts at once, they find that professional support is beneficial. Organizations may become involved with the Counseling Service when, for instance, an employee is working with two different groups needing to share information. When that employee is female, it may be necessary to focus on those interactions rather than the technical issues.

With increasing frequency, the Counseling Service is addressing male and female interactions and also divergent cultural interpretations of situations. For instance, an Asian male supervisor, who traveled frequently, had a female technical staff member maintaining the research when he was out of town. When he returned to the work environment, he reassumed the responsibilities of the project, leaving far less for the technical person to do. Each felt that the other was not recognizing his or her contribution to the research, and the result was that the female became angry, withdrew, and spoke less and less to her supervisor. They had reached a collaborative impasse. When they arrived at the Counseling Service, the woman

---

[67] *Ibid.*

60

described some of her behavior and talked about the work project. The man explained that in his culture when someone ignores a person or withdraws from him/her, it is extremely rude. He could tolerate almost anything but that. By addressing these different interpretations of the situation in a counseling setting, it was possible to break the impasse and get these two people working together again.

Private and confidential sessions offered by the counseling service relate to the specific situation of an individual and can be used in many ways. One example is a young employee who sought support in adapting from the academic environment to the corporate, where expectations are not defined by courses and reinforcement does not come through grades. Directions to young employees to interact, read, and learn about their center and then set up a laboratory can be overwhelming, causing even very talented individuals to freeze. Another example is a woman manager, very competent and respected for her technical skills, who was working part-time with a flexible schedule. She first approached the Counseling Service because of the behavior of one of her technical subordinates, whose lack of interpersonal skills was affecting his career. In the process of developing a plan for this individual, she began to talk about herself, wondering when she should put herself back on the fast track, if this was even possible, and the effect it would have on her family. The opportunity for her to be both part-time and in management was rare. It resulted from the particular composition of her area and of the upper management at AT&T Bell Laboratories.

A specific and unique feature of the Counseling Service at AT&T Bell Laboratories is linkage with a strong and clinically oriented medical department. Each service, counseling and medical, is autonomous and private and confidential. The major advantage of this Health Services Group is the ability to give professional support when a medical problem is a component of a stressful situation.

As a result of its varied involvement with employees, the Counseling Service at AT&T Bell Laboratories has been invited to make presentations to technical women's network organizations, working parents clubs, and groups addressing sexual harassment issues. These informal groupings, which vary from work site to work site, provide avenues for shared information and also for active planning. One of the business units at the AT&T Bell Laboratories planned a full-day program for every unit member with invited speakers and management as participants. Programs such as these have a freshness and energy that help provide employees with encouragement, support, and recognition.

Scios Nova[68]

Scios Nova is a biotechnology company engaged primarily in the development of products for human therapeutic systems. Scios Nova is "known for putting women in positions of responsibility." Early in the company's history, many positions were filled by women, and "the company is predominantly run and managed by women." The field of molecular biology, from which Scios Nova recruits most of its employees, is a relatively new science. Very often, the route to molecular biology is through biochemistry or protein chemistry, two areas that traditionally have attracted women at least in equal numbers to men.[69] Therefore, the fact that Scios Nova hires from a pool of recruits containing higher numbers of women is certainly a contributing factor to the diverse work force in the company. Stephens believes that "future trends for Scios Nova will continue to be in the direction of more women in positions of responsibility, a trend that will be driven by the features of the marketplace."

Scios Nova looks for talent at all levels, without regard to gender, and maintains an aggressive recruitment position of finding the very best person to fill each job. Therefore, offers of employment typically include stock options, a hiring bonus of several thousand dollars, participation in the incentive compensation plan, and financial assistance in relocation or in the purchase of a home.

Scios Nova also has an Employee Referral Program, where an employee is paid $1,000 for every prospective employee referred and subsequently hired. This has been an effective tool in attracting good people. When a new employee is hired into the company, someone from Human Resources discusses with him or her the employee referral program and gets names of potential candidates from other companies.

According to Mr. Stephens, "Scios Nova is proud of its equitable compensation for women and its bonus plan." He reported the following:

---

[68] Drawn from the presentation by Theodore R. Stephens, former director of human resources, Scios Nova, at the CWSE conference, Irvine, CA, January 17, 1993.

[69] Patricia E. White, *op. cit.*

62

- Of the top five highest-paid individuals at Scios Nova, one, the vice-president of finance and administration, is a black woman.
- Twenty individuals in the company are compensated at $90,000 or more per year; nine of them are women.
- Just below that tier of compensation is the $70,000-$90,000 range, which is comprised of 13 individuals, 5 women and 8 men.

In addition to a base salary, employees at Scios Nova earn bonuses, and traditionally women have earned the highest ones. An incentive compensation plan for all employees awards up to 5 percent of an employee's annual base salary. Participants in the senior management incentive compensation plan can earn even more—up to 30 percent of the base salary. Various stock options are part of these incentive payments. Of the 22 individuals eligible for this level of incentive compensation at Scios, 8 are women.

Scios Nova's policies for supporting families will be presented later.

Barrios Technology: A Model Company[70]

Among the examples of programs and initiatives for women managers presented at the CWSE conference, one small company stood out. A relatively small technical company of less than 250 employees that is both woman-owned and woman-managed, Barrios Technology[71] has a strong commitment to moving women into management positions. Women currently occupy 50 percent of management positions, and women are actively encouraged, even aggressively pushed, to move up the management ladder. During their first interview, candidates are told that the company will expect to promote them into management positions. This strategy has

---

[70] Emyre B. Robinson, "Women Scientists and Engineers as Entrepreneurs," presentation at the CWSE conference, Irvine, CA, January 17, 1993.

[71] Emyre B. Robinson is president and Sandra Johnson is chief executive officer of Barrios Technology, located in Houston, TX. In her presentation at the CWSE conference, Deborah Celentano Gerber discussed another small woman-owned/woman-managed company that fits this same description.

resulted in an extremely low attrition rate, a highly loyal and devoted work force, and a profitable and growing company.

The company is also committed to advancement through education. Employees are not only actively encouraged to use the company's tuition reimbursement program, they are given flex-time and part-time options to take advantage of it. Employees are also counseled as to how they can best apply their educational achievements in the workplace.

The company has an active mentorship program. Every woman has a mentor, either self-selected or assigned. The mentor is responsible for teaching the protegé how to progress in the company, encouraging her to take risks, and fully supporting her with appropriate training. The mentor is encouraged to bring the protegé on assignments and include her in the planning processes that occur. Mentors are given financial rewards, compensatory time, and other incentives to encourage them to meet with their protegés.

If employees are promoted into management positions in which they find their new responsibilities to be beyond their capabilities, the company tries to provide direction. The two chief administrators maintain a policy of constant accessibility not only to the people who work directly under them, but also to those at office sites. The company sends managers to short-term personal enterprise programs and a university marketing program.

The company also looks for innovative ways to solve problems. For example, the office in New Mexico was experiencing problems with a white male manager in an office comprising mostly women and Hispanics. The manager left the company, whereupon two people were promoted to take his place—an Hispanic male and a white female. These individuals determined the aspects of management at which they were most proficient and split the responsibilities along those lines. The situation was successfully resolved because senior management was committed to trying an alternative method and to backing up the people involved until they had a chance to work through the problem.

The company applies the same flexibility to work-family issues. Parental leave is granted to men as well as women when a baby is born. Parents can bring the infant to work, and the company will arrange on-site day care when needed. The president of the company believes this does not have a negative impact on productivity. Teamwork and shared responsibility for decision making are promoted, so that if someone needs

64

to take a leave of absence for family or health reasons, others in the group assume his/her responsibilities temporarily.

The company does not tolerate harassment of any kind and immediately addresses it on a personal level. It "has had some problems with older males in the past," but addressed them by bringing in outside management consultants.[72]

Elements of Effective Programs

Companies have found that recruitment and retention of their technical work force are improved when the company has undertaken steps to ensure the following:

- exciting and personally satisfying work;
- viable and diverse technical and management career paths; and
- educational opportunities, both at the corporate site and at local colleges and universities, that develop leadership and technical expertise.

Retention of women scientists and engineers is further enhanced by

- flexible schedules established as formal corporate policies with support from management,
- programs of reward and recognition,[73] and
- family leave programs.

To address the issues of recruitment and retention, DuPont established a Work and Family Committee. Similarly, Corning Inc. and Hughes Aircraft have corporate units that address these issues.[74] By

---

[72] Emyre Robinson, *op. cit.*

[73] Barbara Link, manager of applications engineering at GE Aircraft Engines, speaking at the CWSE conference, Irvine, CA, January 17, 1993.

[74] A detailed description of these programs is given by Esther M. Conwell, "Promoting Science and Engineering Careers in Industry," in

supporting women's groups with access to top executives for presentation of issues and discussion of both problems and positive gains, these companies have significantly improved the work environment for women.

Another example of action on these issues is provided by Argonne National Laboratory (ANL), a government-owned, corporate-operated (GO-CO) facility where many programs for professional women exist.[75] To organize its annual conference on issues confronting women pursuing technological careers, Argonne created a special position, Women in Science Program Initiator: the incumbent devotes approximately 30 percent of her time to the conference. One's assignment in this position lasts 2-3 years, and the position is then rotated to another woman scientist employed at ANL.

An overriding theme heard throughout the CWSE-sponsored conference was the importance of enlightened top management. Changes needed to hire and retain women scientists and engineers will not be fully realized unless the CEO is committed to hiring women and developing a climate where women thrive. That this is true has been shown in a variety of companies, particularly those described earlier in this report. During the January 1993 conference, several practicing scientists and engineers reflected on the difficult atmosphere in companies where dialogue with top executives is absent. Men, as well as women, find this detrimental to their career advancement.

When Catalyst asked female engineers to suggest improvements in the culture of their corporations, their strongest suggestion was that top management must be supportive of removing the obstacles to women's advancement.[76] CEOs and managers must lead the way in changing the

---

Marsha Lakes Matyas and Linda Skidmore Dix (eds.), *Science and Engineering Programs: On Target for Women?,* Washington, DC: National Academy Press, 1992.

[75] Linda Skidmore Dix, "Promoting Careers in the Federal Government," in Marsha Lakes Matyas and Linda Skidmore Dix (eds.), *Science and Engineering Programs: On Target for Women?,* Washington, D.C.: National Academy Press, 1992.

[76] Marion Yuen, director of advisory services, Catalyst Inc., presentation at the CWSE conference, Irvine, CA, January 17, 1993.

cultural environment in the corporate engineering workplace. At the same time, women themselves must realize the importance of becoming role models for the women coming after them and of recruiting women into the engineering workplace. If a company has a reputation for hiring women and being supportive of them and this is publicized, women will want to come and work for that company.[77]

In addition to the involvement of upper management in developing a receptive climate, U.S. companies are targeting specific areas that affect their attractiveness to women scientists and engineers: recruitment initiatives, career development, mentoring, professional networks, compensation and bonuses, and work-family issues. Each is described more fully below.

Well-Developed Recruitment Initiatives

According to Ronnie Cresswell, vice-president and chairman of Parke-Davis Pharmaceutical Research,

> . . . Our success depends on the caliber of people that we employ. As we plan for the future of the company, our greatest challenge is to create an environment that will attract and retain the most talented people. To do this, we must *recruit* from the entire population of talent and allow each colleague the opportunity to reach her/his full potential.[78]

The identification and recruitment of scientists and engineers, both women and men, occur through various initiatives. Many conference participants

---

[77] *Ibid.*

[78] Ronnie Cresswell, vice president and chairman, Parke-Davis Pharmaceutical Research, in "Career Development," pamphlet from the Parke-Davis Career Development Committee, 1992. According to Eugenia Kunzman, a scientist in the Genetics Toxicology Department at Parke-Davis, the company's Career Development Committee is "a grass-roots group of scientists and administrators dedicated to helping all employees, especially women and minorities, with career development."

agreed with the summary of Barbara Link, a manager at General Electric, about effective recruitment approaches, which center around six elements:

1   The recruiters are engineers, scientists, and managers of engineers and scientists, not the Human Resources Division representatives.
2   Employees chosen as corporate recruiters are those who exhibit strong interpersonal skills, who "care and go the extra mile."
3   Recruitment occurs at a targeted group of universities.
4   The company maintains a corporate presence on each campus, interacting with faculty, students, and staff.
5   Entry-level recruits rotate through a series of technical and management assignments to learn about program opportunities.
6   Co-op programs enable the company to evaluate potential employees while they pursue projects that support the work of the GE laboratories.

Additional linkages with universities have been developed by many companies to identify prospective employees. Examples are provided by the programs at ALCOA and AT&T Bell Laboratories described earlier.

Career Development

Many U.S. companies have aggressively begun to provide incentives for women scientists and engineers to join and to remain in their work forces. At Parke-Davis Pharmaceutical Research, for instance,

> [e]ach manager is accountable for ensuring diversity at all levels in her/his area. Colleagues, as well, are responsible for strengthening the skills of the women in their areas. The Career Development Committee works with Human Resources to raise awareness of possible barriers, inspire colleagues, and provide opportunities for career growth.[79]

Career development should begin as soon as a person is employed by a company. For example, Intel's Graduate Rotation Program provides

---

[79] *Ibid.*

an opportunity for new employees to work in four different areas of the company—such as processing engineering—each for a three-month period, before beginning employment in the specific department for which they were hired. According to George Leach, a design manager at Intel, individuals participating in this program "have the increased confidence, experience and contacts to perform in an outstanding manner."[80]

As reported from a survey of women engineers, "Active career development programs, whether targeted specifically for women or for employees in general, are beneficial to women."[81] Diversity training is also valuable, and participation in such training could be one of the key items on which managers are evaluated in performance reviews along with their success in hiring females and underrepresented minorities. The role of supervisors in career development is also important. Conference participants stressed that supervisors are key to recognition and reward and, therefore, to career development.

Corporations recognizing that getting the best person for the job is important for the bottom line consider women as well as men for management positions. However, having few women in significant managerial positions can affect the ability of corporations to recruit women. Moreover, women in technical management have access to corporate power and resources and can help to create career opportunities for women. By using the resources of the organization, they can influence the number of positions available for technical women; the nature of those positions; the range of internal corporate programs, such as career guidance efforts; and the establishment of outside relationships, such as university partnerships.

Therefore, many companies are creating programs and initiatives that encourage women to enter the management career ladder and to make steady progress up that ladder. For instance, corporations can create various managerial opportunities for their employees, depending on the organizational style of the company and the goals of the individual. In standard matrix management, there is, in addition to the typical line

---

[80] Charlene Johnson and Irinnie Arriola, Getting a good look at Intel, *Innovator* 4(104):10-11, 1991.

[81] Deborah Celentano Gerber, *op. cit.*

management, project management, wherein individuals manage tasks—some as large as $50 million contracts—but none of the people in that program report to them in a supervisory sense. Project managers are not responsible for performance reviews and listening to complaints about management. Instead they focus on the task. The technical parallel scale in a company employing matrix management generally goes up quite high, and those at the top level are called fellows. A high level of prestige is reportedly associated with these positions, and their salary ranges are the same as those of individuals in comparable managerial jobs.

Such changes in corporate opportunities, policies, and programs have profoundly affected the numbers of women in management, including:

- From 1986 to 1991, the percentage of women on the design staff at General Motors Corporation increased from 8 to 12 percent of the total engineering work force.[82]
- From 1984 to 1989, the percentage of women scientific managers at AT&T increased from 3.6 percent to 5 percent.[83]
- In 1992, two-thirds of promotions to management at DuPont went to white men, 33 percent to women, and about 15 percent to people of color. At DuPont (U.S.), women and people of color comprise 26 percent of the exempt work force (i.e., those not qualifying for overtime pay, a category into which managers, scientists, and engineers usually fall). This compares to national statistics that saw women and people of color comprising 25 percent of the exempt work force.[84]
- Women comprise 20 percent of the engineers and technicians at

[82] Maria Quintana, presentation at the CWSE conference, Irvine, CA, January 17, 1993.

[83] Emily T. Smith, Alice LaPlante, Paul Angiolillo, and Catherine L. Cantrell, The women who are scaling high tech's heights, *Business Week* **3121**:86-88, August 28, 1989.

[84] Deborah Grubbe, engineering manager, Specialty Chemicals, DuPont, speaking at the CWSE conference, Irvine, CA, January 17, 1993.

Loral Infrared and Imaging Systems,[85] in comparison to their comprising 8 percent of the total U.S. engineering work force.[86]

• Women are CEOs at 3 percent of the 25,000 small companies in the health services and electronics industries.[87]

Nevertheless,

There is a glass ceiling in most companies, and we're trying to figure out how to break it. If it was easy, we'd have done it by now.[88]

At the same time, however, many U.S. companies, particularly those in defense-related industries, are decreasing the size of their work forces. One adverse effect of this downsizing (termed "right-sizing" by some companies such as ALCOA) is that women new to the work force may find their employment terminated if retention is based on seniority with their current employers. Thus, career development programs may involve fewer women until the economy in general and the work force in defense-related companies in particular become more stable.

Mentoring Programs

"A Study of Occupational Departure of Employees in the Natural Sciences and Engineering" conducted by Anne Preston[89] revealed that women who developed successful S&E careers, almost without exception, had important mentors who encouraged them, provided them support, and

---

[85] Jill Wittels, *op. cit.*

[86] U.S. Department of Labor, Bureau of Labor Statistics, unpublished data from Current Population Survey 1992.

[87] Emily T. Smith, *op. cit.*

[88] Ed McCracken, CEO of Silicon Graphics Computer Systems, quoted in *Upside,* January 1993.

[89] See Chapter I for more information about this study.

steered them through the early phases of their careers. For many women, exit occurred at times of uncertainty and doubt, times when mentoring could have made a difference and possibly prevented the exit.

Mentoring need not be provided by a woman, and in most cases it is not. However, women talked about the value of having a strong female role model. Mentors are most valuable if they are on the same career track as their protegés and if they have day-to-day contact with protegés in the early stages of their careers. Although a mentoring relationship is important for all individuals launching a career in science and engineering, it may be more important for women because women scientists and engineers are entering a male-dominated workplace and violating traditional social patterns for women. Dr. Preston reported,

> Individuals with bachelor's and master's degrees usually look for a career outside academe, so professors are not as valuable to them in terms of mentoring. However, after a woman enters the [industrial] work force and is finding her way in a male-dominated workplace, it is especially important to find a mentor—a supervisor or colleague—who can help her develop confidence and skills.[90]

Throughout the CWSE conference, career women concurred with Dr. Preston's assessment of the importance of attracting young women to industry as scientists and engineers by mentoring that is provided from women already pursuing careers in science and engineering. Professional women must be willing to serve as role models; to develop programs; and to speak about career opportunities, advise, and mentor. (Of course, the downside to this is that, because there are fewer women than men in S&E jobs in industry, senior women tend to devote more time to mentoring younger women than their male counterparts who mentor younger men.) At the same time, it is impractical for either the scientist/engineer or the employer to require that one hold a full-time position and devote significant amounts of one's "own" time to serving as a mentor for others, both women and men. As a result, the management in some companies have developed policies that reward their employees, both women and men,

---

[90] Anne Preston, *op. cit.*

72

who serve as role models and mentors. More scientists and engineers might be willing to advise less experienced individuals in the technical ranks if the contributions to corporate productivity realized by such mentoring programs were recognized by management.

Another approach is for professional women to retain contact with colleges and universities by becoming adjunct professors and advising students. At New Mexico State University, the Indian Resource Development Program encourages and assists Native American high school students to go into the fields of engineering, business, and agriculture.[91] The American Indian Science and Engineering Society, in existence for 15 years now, also supports Native American students in science and engineering and actively works to increase their numbers in industry.[92]

It is important to realize that mentor-protegé relationships may change with time. For instance, a mentor may eventually become one's peer, and the transition may be difficult for both parties. The former mentor may seem too paternalistic, and the former protegé may no longer want that kind of relationship.

It seems to be more difficult to find effective mentors as a woman moves up in a company and as the pyramid narrows. This is also the case for a man. Some of the best mentors may not be in one's own direct chain of command. They might be in another area, and it may take more effort to maintain the mentor-protegé relationship in these cases. Immediate supervisors can make very good mentors, but there is always the difficulty of knowing when the person is functioning as a boss or as a mentor. It is important to track both of those relationships and to handle them correctly.

As a woman moves up in a corporation, the more people she will mentor at all levels, of both sexes, and even in other organizations. One manager stated that she takes a special interest in the women she mentors, but she is also very deliberate about mentoring key, talented males for two reasons. First, they are important to the success of the organization, and, second, she wants to be judged as being fair to all employees.

---

[91] For information, contact Lance Lujan, Director, Indian Resource Development Center, Box 30001, Department 3IRD, New Mexico State University, Las Cruces, NM 88003.

[92] For information, contact Norbert S. Hill Jr., Executive Director, American Indian Science and Engineering Society (AISES), 1630 30th Street—Suite 301, Boulder, Colorado 80301.

A summary of the elements of an effective mentoring program was provided by Pamela Atkinson, director of televised instruction in engineering at the College of Engineering, University of California-Berkeley:

- It has support from the very top of the company but cannot depend on just one person's strength of personality.
- Hard money is important for getting the program going; ideally, a mentoring program should be a line item in the budget.
- The program ties to the company's goals. It is related to how the company is going to succeed in whatever it does, whatever it sells.
- The program has an administrative staff to run it.
- The mentors are rewarded in some way. While enhanced organizational performance in itself is a reward, recognition of his or her role in that achievement often maintains a mentor's interest.
- The program is tailored to the group for which it is set up.
- The program is evaluated and revised regularly.[93]

Women's Networks

Often women are not aware of how their own behaviors and attitudes may hinder their advancement. Women's networks have been found to be effective ways for women to learn from each other, mentor each other, and generally "learn the system." In addition, networks are a means for "women interested in changing jobs . . . to let others know of their availability.[94]

Corporate Networks. The best approach for women's networks appears to be one that focuses on business needs. For example, through mentoring

---

[93] Other elements of effective mentoring programs were described in an earlier conference sponsored by CWSE and reported by Mildred S. Dresselhaus and Linda Skidmore Dix, "Summary: Cross-Cutting Issues," in Marsha Lakes Matyas and Linda Skidmore Dix (eds.), *Science and Engineering Programs: On Target for Women?*, Washington, DC: National Academy Press, 1992.

[94] Jane S. Allen, *op. cit.*

activities, a network can help to improve retention; or by sponsoring career days, it can improve hiring. This focus will help the network succeed and be viewed by upper management as a valuable, positive program. Such networks should include men: most important jobs are still filled by men, and some of those men have attitudes supportive of women's advancement in science and engineering. Successful examples of women's networks are the programs established by companies such as Corning Inc. and Hughes Aircraft Company.[95]

Corporations can help women managers by encouraging the formation of women's groups to address their concerns as well as mainstream business issues. Sometimes these meetings may deal principally with business in order to help everyone become informed—for example, about how business is doing in another division, what is happening in development, and what the sales figures are. The Women Managers Roundtable at Xerox, discussed earlier in this chapter, was set up by Paul Allaire, CEO of the corporation, to report on how the company is doing concerning recruitment, retention, and other issues of concern to women employees.

When women are attempting to take their case forward in the company on a particular issue, it is helpful to show evidence that a body outside the company on a national level has embraced a particular strategy with positive results. Most managers are willing to make changes, but they feel unqualified to take the lead, or they are unwilling to try something new for fear it may have negative consequences.

Particularly if the company appears negatively entrenched in its thinking regarding minorities and women, advocacy groups must be careful not to offend or anger the people with power in the company. Many conference participants involved in women's networks noted that an advocacy group must focus primarily on educating in a way that does not create a defensive reaction, and how forceful the group wants to be must be gauged by what will make the most progress at a particular point in

---

[95] Esther M. Conwell, "Promoting Science and Engineering Careers in Industry," in Marsha Lakes Matyas and Linda Skidmore Dix (eds.), *Science and Engineering Programs: On Target for Women?*, Washington, DC: National Academy Press, 1992.

time.[96] Catalyst maintains a data base of corporate women's groups and has promoted the formation of such groups but finds little support for such activities in many corporations. Often management fails to see the benefits of such groups, and women themselves are somewhat hesitant to join women's networks because they fear a negative impact on their careers due to management perceptions or because they feel these groups could become time sinks. It is often necessary to balance shorter-term personal goals and longer-term group goals. In the former connection it may be noted that some women reported that their managers did not approve of their attendance at the CWSE-sponsored conference; others said they could not speak candidly because it would result in trouble from their management.

Women's advocacy groups or networks can sometimes be a difficult issue for the woman manager because she must carefully balance her roles as woman employee and company manager.

Professional Networks. Networking can link entry-level scientists and engineers with more experienced individuals who share their experiences and offer advice, specifically in the area of career advancement.[97] Professional networking encourages the sharing of information and helps women to feel that they are supported in their pursuit of careers that have not traditionally been open to them. For example, Systers is a network begun in October 1987 "to aid communication among women interested in 'systems,' thus the name 'systers,'" according to the electronic network's originator, Anita Borg.[98]

---

[96] Carolyn Leighton, founding executive director, International Network of Women in Technology (WITI), and president, Criterion Research, speaking at the CWSE conference, Irvine, CA, January 17, 1993.

[97] Harriet Kagiwada, in Marsha Lakes Matyas and Linda S. Dix (eds.), *Science and Engineering Programs: On Target for Women?*, Washington, DC: National Academy Press, 1992.

[98] Personal electronic communication to Linda Skidmore, January 25, 1993. More information about Systers can be obtained from Dr. Borg via Bitnet: borg@pa.dec.com or by mail: Network Systems Laboratory, Digital Equipment Corporation, 250 University Avenue, Palo Alto, CA 94301.

Networking within professional societies also helps women to expand their knowledge and skills beyond their specific areas, to develop leadership skills, and to have a broader impact by participating in professional meetings, including their company.[99] Generally, if women are not active in the organization of professional meetings, they tend to be underrepresented as presenters and even as attendees. The American Chemical Society (ACS), for example, encourages participation by women at all levels of its organization and attempts to have them actively involved in ACS meetings and conferences, beginning at the local level. In fact, the Women Chemists Committee of ACS publishes a monthly newsletter that informs chemists about work-force trends, "hot topics" in the field, sources of research funding, and meeting updates. Work-force statistics compiled by ACS show that

> women chemists have made some progress in the field of chemistry over the past decade and a half. The number of degrees in chemistry going to women has increased in all degree levels, the fraction of women who are chemists has increased, and women's salaries relative to men's have increased a little.[100]

The American Institute of Physics (AIP) has many mechanisms for assisting its members, both women and men. For instance, AIP regularly publishes data about education and employment in physics.[101] Such information can guide the career direction of both students and degreed physicists.

---

[99]Harriet Kagiwada, *op. cit.*

[100]American Chemical Society, *Domestic Status, Discrimination, and Career Opportunities of Men and Women Chemists: A Report of the American Chemical Society's 1991 Survey of Domestic Status, Employment, and Attitudes of Men and Women ACS Members*, Washington, DC: ACS, October 1992.

[101]See, for instance, Susanne D. Ellis and Patrick J. Mulvey, *Employment Survey 1991* (AIP Pub. No. R-282.15), New York: American Institute of Physics, October 1992.

A sampling of other professional organizations involved with promoting minority women as scientists and engineers and their work includes the following:

- The American Physiological Society's Mentoring Program is designed to quickly integrate women into the physiology research community by matching female graduate students, postdoctoral fellows, junior faculty members, and first entrants to industry positions with female and male mentors in their subfield.
- The National Organization for the Professional Advancement of Black Chemists and Chemical Engineers supports many initiatives, particularly the design and implementation of educational programs for minority students.
- The American Society for Mechanical Engineering established a joint Board on Minorities and Women about three years ago with the objective of attracting, retaining, and promoting minorities and women within the society.
- The National Technical Association promotes professional networking among African American scientists and engineers through periodicals and conferences.
- The National Action Council for Minorities in Engineering increases access to engineering careers for African American, Hispanic, and Native American men and women through research and public policy analysis, publications, educational program development, and scholarship support.
- There are also a Society of Hispanic Professional Engineers and an American Indian Science and Engineering Society.

Those who have already embarked on a career path also find professional societies useful for help in moving in a particular direction in their career or for getting lateral-type experience.[102] Conferences that bring professionals——men and women, minorities or white——together are also an important way to empower them. In fact, such opportunities for networking have been shown to be so important that the Association of American Colleges has stated that they should be

---

[102] Harriet Kagiwada, former president of Sigma Delta Epsilon, speaking at the CWSE conference on interventions, Irvine, California, November 4, 1991.

an established part of annual meetings and other events where junior and senior people are likely to be brought together.[103]

Compensation and Bonuses

Salaries and bonuses can have a strong influence on the retention of women as well as men. However, as noted earlier, women scientists and engineers in industry, as in all employment sectors, tend to have lower salaries than their male counterparts. A number of companies are beginning to recognize that disparities of this nature may exist. A few companies, often spurred by women's advocacy groups, have initiated studies to gather critical data and to address inequalities, if found. An illustrative example is provided by Xerox: the Xerox Women's Council (referred to earlier) chose salary equity as one of the possible problem areas to be addressed. On request, the Council received from the company salary data for professionals in Xerox laboratories including grade, age, and years in grade. Names, of course, were not supplied. Upon examination of the data, with answers provided to questions about a few of the cases, the Council concluded that there was reasonable salary equity.

Addressing Work-Family Issues

Some companies whose employees attended the CWSE conference, as well as other U.S. corporations, have instituted programs to facilitate balance between work and family responsibilities. For instance, several companies in the San Francisco area are "training managers to be more family-friendly."[104] In addition, some U.S. companies have established Work and Family Committees to aid in the retention of talented employees. Some examples follow.

---

[103] Roberta M. Hall and Bernice R. Sandler, *Academic Mentoring for Women Students and Faculty: A New Look at an Old Way to Get Ahead,* Washington, DC: Association of American Colleges, Project on the Status and Education of Women, 1983.

[104] Sue Shellenbarger, Work & family, *The Wall Street Journal,* May 19, 1993.

At the ALCOA Technical Center, a Work-Family Issues Committee was charged with developing recommendations to address these issues and to implement, with management approval, policies and programs to assist employees in balancing work and family. ALCOA now has in place a comprehensive program, including the following:[105]

- flexible work hours, where employees can adjust their arrival and departure times as well as lunch times—which can be from 30 minutes to two hours in length;
- staggered work schedules, with the authorization of a supervisor, so long as the employee works 40 hours per week;
- excused absence, at the discretion of a supervisor, to handle personal emergencies or unpredictable situations;
- unpaid personal leave for family-related matters or other circumstances requiring time away from work, up to a maximum of 6 weeks per year;
- part-time employment, for employees with at least one year of continuous service and demonstrated good performance, for a period not to exceed three years;
- vacation carryover of up to one-fourth of unused vacation per year;
- on-site seminars for employees with dependent-care responsibilities (e.g., surviving toddlerhood, balancing work and family, support and care for elderly parents); and
- the child-care referral program, funded by ALCOA Technical Center and operated by the Child Care Network, a United Way agency. This program helps employees locate caregivers near their home or workplace, educates employees on the selection of quality child care, provides workshops on child care and parenting issues, provides resource data on currently operating child care facilities in the area, and locates summer care for school-age children.[106]

---

[105] A similar program is in place at Corning. See Esther M. Conwell, *op. cit.*

[106] Ophelia R. Scott, *op. cit.*

Aerospace Corporation has undertaken several initiatives to help its employees achieve a balance between family and work responsibilities.[107] For instance, provision for maternity leave was developed by the Women's Committee long before California state law required it. This leave has been taken by many women, and there is also the option to extend it by three months. Although a family leave policy is not yet in place, one is being developed. Aerospace also instituted a lactation program several years ago that has been positively received and very helpful in giving mothers the ability to continue nursing their babies. A child-care referral program operates at Aerospace, but there is no child-care facility. The increased number of outside facilities offering this service, however, make this less of an issue than it was five years ago. Finally, part-time employment and flexible scheduling both occur at Aerospace, but the flex-time is not as flexible as at many companies: an hour is allowed on either end of the day for flexible scheduling, which seems inadequate for many women who must pick up or deliver children to child-care centers.

AT&T Bell Laboratories has a number of flexible programs for its employees, including child care resources, family leave, flexible excused workdays, management personal days, leave for the care of newborn or newly adopted child, leave for family care, School Smart (which helps employees with educational issues for school-aged children), a family care development fund, adoption resource and referral, and child care and elder care reimbursement programs. They also have a lactation program similar to that of Aerospace.

Scios Nova also has developed a number of policies and benefits to encourage and support families. The maternity policy compensates employees for 90 days at full salary, provided the doctor prescribes a leave of absence beyond the standard 6 weeks. An additional month or two can be taken off without pay, and during that time all benefits are paid by the company. Due to the size of the company, Scios Nova does not provide an on-site child care center; nor does it have a policy on child care. However, it does provide employees the opportunity to set aside pretax dollars through flexible spending accounts to help defray some of the costs of child care, and it also directs employees to several organizations in the San Francisco Bay area that assist parents in finding suitable day care.

---

[107] Shirley McCarty, *op. cit.*

It has been reported that as many as 10 percent of U.S. "companies are using new strategies to address employees' child-care problems."[108] On-site child-care centers have been built by a few large U.S. companies, while others, such as Schering-Plough, provide child-care subsidies to their employees.

Addressing Attrition

The turnover rate of females and minorities with high potential in many companies is high relative to that of white men. Some of those women get better employment offers elsewhere, which is good, especially if they "ditch a less promising company," reported one physicist employed in industry. However, according to James F. Kearns, executive vice-president in DuPont's Fibers Division, "Some of them [females] apparently are not confident that they will have opportunities in line with their talents."[109] Companies that are committed to a diverse work force and the retention of women and minorities are beginning to study this issue, for it is important to learn whether the higher turnover rate of women scientists and engineers is a sign of a problem or a solution. As Kearns noted,

> If we don't do a better job of communicating how we're working on this, some may leave because they think the company just doesn't care.

What are companies doing to halt such perceptions and low retention of women? An example is given by ALCOA Technical Center. The Center formed a retention team to quantify retention of minority and female scientists and engineers, perform cause-and-effect analyses, determine root and/or contributing causes, and compare the findings with similar measures and issues for the majority population at ALCOA Technical Center, so the causes could be classified on some shared unique scale. Following data analysis that showed strong evidence of higher

---

[108] Sue Shellenbarger, Work & family, *The Wall Street Journal,* May 19, 1993.

[109] DuPont, *op. cit.*

82

attrition among females and minorities, the retention team engaged an independent consultant to interview current and former employees to identify issues causing or contributing to terminations. Upper management has received the consultant's findings, and the retention team is currently preparing recommendations to address the issues contributing to termination.

Evaluation of Programs

With the broad range of programs offered to enhance recruitment and retention, some corporations are seeking ways to evaluate their programs in an effort to maximize their return. For example, ALCOA Technical Company has formed teams of employees to evaluate and, as needed, improve the programs. The numbers of females and minorities hired and participants in the Summer Professional Employment Program are monitored. After the flexible work schedule and family leave policies have been operational for several years, their effectiveness will be measured by such factors as productivity of workers, rates of absenteeism, returns from maternity leave, and number of employees opting for part-time employment. Meanwhile, ALCOA Technical Center continues to educate supervisors and managers on the flexible options and also on the activities of the Work-Family Issues Committee. As managers gain more knowledge of the policies and their application, it is hoped that they will encourage and support employees in their use of the flexible options. As more employees seek ways to manage work and family, the Work-Family Issues Committee expects to explore permanent part-time employment, job sharing, and excused-absence days for caring for sick family members. Additionally, as ALCOA streamlines its work force, permanent part-time employment and job sharing may be options to aid work-force reductions.[110]

Another example is provided by Corning Inc. Finding a lower retention rate for women and lower job satisfaction among women than men, in 1987 Corning set up what it called a Corrective Action Team. On the recommendation of this team, a number of actions were carried out similar to those listed above for the ALCOA Technical Center, as well as mentoring and counseling programs and a new career planning system. In

---

[110] Ophelia R. Scott, *op. cit.*

tracking the results of these actions, the company found that by 1991 the attrition rate of women at Corning had decreased by more than a factor of 3, coming close to the attrition rate for men.[111] It is noteworthy that the attrition rate for men had also dropped in this period.

The feedback and continuing activities built into the ALCOA program and the ability to track the results of actions built into the Xerox program are important illustrations of the necessity and utility of program evaluation.

The available statistics bolstered by the examples presented in this chapter, clearly indicate the need for two things. One, mentioned earlier, is accurate data on the status of women in science and engineering employed in industry on both an individual-company and industry-wide basis; this is critical to policy formulation. Second, the examples of corporate initiatives brought forth at the conference suggest the need for a compilation of as many "successful" programs as possible and a culling of the most important attributes of these programs to inform strategies and policies that address the underrepresentation of women in science and engineering in industry, as well as women's career development issues in industry.

---

[111] For further details, see Esther M. Conwell, *op. cit.*

Metta Tanikawa takes measurements on an experimental weather station on a rooftop at the Air Force Space and Missile Systems Center.
(Photo: The Aerospace Corporation)

IV. ATTRIBUTES AND STRATEGIES
FOR SUCCESSFUL EMPLOYMENT IN INDUSTRY

Although not designated as an agenda topic, the attributes and strategies of women who attain successful careers in the sciences and engineering were discussed in most sessions at the conference sponsored by the Committee on Women in Science and Engineering (CWSE). In this chapter, both general characteristics of industrially employed women scientists and engineers and those specific to women managers and entrepreneurs in technology-based companies are summarized.

In contrast to Murphy's law is a guide presented at the CWSE conference by James W. Mitchell to women scientists and engineers seeking industrial employment:

- Make your decision to join the corporate sector a deliberate one.
- Construct a personal agenda that embodies 5-year plans focusing on monthly objectives and annual reviews of accomplishments as well as a commitment to industrial employment for at least a decade.
- Develop fine-tuned leadership skills that encompass communication, people-interaction dynamics, and networking.
- Analyze, understand, and exploit institutional dynamics.[112]

General Characteristics

Five attributes appear to be common to women who have earned S&E degrees and successfully pursued industrial employment—whether as practicing scientists and engineers, managers of scientists and engineers, or entrepreneurs in science- and engineering-based companies. Those qualities are (1) S&E expertise and competence, (2) the ability to establish and meet goals and to take risks, (3) strong communication skills, (4) self-confidence, and (5) openness to change.

---

[112] James W. Mitchell, "Industrial Science and Engineering Careers: Successful Longevity," presentation at the CWSE conference, Irvine, CA, January 17, 1993.

S&E Expertise and Competence

A strong technical or scientific background and thorough hands-on experience early in one's career are equally important for women and men in advancing their industrial careers. Much has been said about women feeling frustrated by a glass ceiling, "not a physical barrier erected by ill-intended CEOs [but] rather an attitudinal hurdle consisting of unconscious stereotypes and perceptions."[113] In addition, conference participants were concerned about the existence of "glass walls" inhibiting lateral movement. A number of studies, notably the one by Catalyst, have made the point that lateral moves are important in career development.[114] Lateral moves are often developmental assignments that challenge employees to take risks by moving into new areas of the business and learning new skills. A Families and Work Institute survey showed that women and men reported approximately the same number of vertical career moves.[115] However, more men than women reported that they had had both vertical and lateral moves. This finding suggests that more needs to be done to make lateral development assignments available to women at all stages of their careers and to communicate to women the importance of accepting these sometimes risky assignments.

Technical competence is also the foundation for good manage-magnet, and it includes not only a woman's own technical competence but also being respectful of the competencies of others. Not only must a woman manager be very good at what she does, she must also align her expectations with her abilities. This process must be continuous, taking into account changes in one's abilities, interests, and opportunities. A woman in a technical field needs to continue learning all her life, both how to excel in her specialty and how to be a manager if she goes into management. The same holds for men also, of course.

The effective manager also knows that the skills that are most important for a manager are different from the skills that are most

---

[113] Paula A. Graham, a technical manager, presentation at the CWSE conference, Irvine, CA, January 17, 1993.

[114] Marion Yuen, *op. cit.*

[115] Arlene Johnson, *op. cit.*

important for a practicing scientist or engineer. How one spends time and derives satisfaction at work are also different for managers than for practicing scientists and engineers. Therefore, even if a corporation encourages a woman to become a manager, she should do it only if she is willing to spend her time and derive her satisfaction from management. Furthermore, a woman's aptitude for and interest in management can change with time. As she grows older and matures, she might become more interested in management, as is often the case with men. Therefore, it is important that she keep her expectations and abilities aligned and inform her supervisors, at any given stage, what she thinks she is capable of doing and would like to do next, in the context of serving the company.

An important part of competence in management is trusting one's own instincts. Managers make many decisions based on whatever data are available, on personal knowledge, and on their own instincts. At the CWSE conference, a vice-president of engineering described instincts in management as parallel to technical intuition:

> Technical skills can be learned. Very early in [your] career you make predictions about how technical experiments will come out; you analyze data, look at the results, see if your intuition was right. If it wasn't, you change your hypothesis and start again. Management skills are similar. . . . When I mentor people, I often pose a management problem and ask what they would do. We discuss the problem, and later on I tell them what I did or what some other manager did and what the outcome was. Women interested in management can begin to train themselves in this same way.[116]

Without developing instincts that she can trust and rely on, a woman may not have the confidence necessary to take risks and make the decisions needed in a management job. Developing those instincts becomes more and more important as a manager advances to increasingly responsible positions.

---

[116] Jill Wittels, *op. cit.*

Ability To Establish Goals and To Take Risks

Many participants felt that successful women scientists and engineers in industry have personal inner strength that is necessary to combat the pressures they may encounter in their careers. In general, from a young age, women in the United States are trained to follow the rules, to take few risks. This societal programming has many implications for a woman's choice of career. Women who overcome the many cultural barriers to pursuing a technical career in industry often display a strength of character and willingness to take risks, despite outside pressure.

Risk taking may continue throughout a career in industry. There is no guarantee that employees will have their jobs next week or next year. A scientist or engineer may begin a particular line of work but later be assigned elsewhere. One who chooses employment in industry must be both flexible and willing to change career direction.

Conference participants advised women scientists and engineers to use their current situations to their full advantage. The founder of a high-tech company called this "getting involved in company politics," a term that she does not consider derogatory:

> Every company has it, and you have to know who the best technical people are, who the most influential people are, who can give you the best advice, and who can help you get ahead. Tell your supervisor and manager what your goals are, because this knowledge will help them to assist you [in] meeting those goals.[117]

Furthermore,

> If women start playing office politics and get into positions where they are higher on the career ladders, perhaps they can change some of the corporate structure and integrate some different hierarchies of corporations and different ways of acting and addressing issues.[118]

---

[117] Emyre B. Robinson, *op. cit.*

[118] Rae Ann Hallstrom, *op. cit.*

90

Setting goals, both realistic and ambitious, takes practice. Learning how to set goals that are important to one's company may require discussing possible goals with peers and supervisors. Such a discussion with one's boss can be helpful not only in learning how to set goals, but also in learning more about the company's prospects, needs, and priorities.

Strong Communication Skills

Communication skills are important in all work settings, but especially so in industry where there is a strong team ethic:

> In today's high-technology companies, teamwork is the key to developing technological products and bringing them to market, they say. And effective teamwork requires the ability to communicate both vertically and horizontally through an organization. As a result, interpersonal skills are almost as important as technical competence.[119]

Both research scientists and managers must be able to express themselves clearly and succinctly to supervisors as well as subordinates. This includes articulating desires—for example, for a better performance review or a promotion—in an acceptable way. Developing strong communication skills is essential for obtaining recognition and respect for one's work; one must not hesitate to "speak out to promote oneself, make oneself visible to upper management by letting them know what you have to offer the company and what you have accomplished."[120] Some assertiveness and courage are required, but assertiveness may be difficult for some women.

At the conference, S&E managers noted that, too often, women assume that somehow upper management should know what they want. This is not the case. As one manager put it, "Many times in my career,

---

[119] Lisa J. Bain, Judging interpersonal skills is key to hiring in industry, *The Scientist,* February 8, 1993.

[120] Eugenia Kunzman, *op. cit.*

being very explicit with my boss about wanting a particular job was the biggest factor in getting the job."[121] Another conference participant, a computer scientist, reported that she was told by her manager to find 10 different ways of telling her story, because she would have 10 different audiences and she needed to reach all of them. She asserts that she has learned to speak up to management and feels that, in general, she has not been penalized for making known to management some of the important issues that she has faced as a woman in industry.

Communication with one's subordinates also is important, and managers can never give enough positive feedback. Positive feedback is invaluable for encouraging and motivating employees; and receiving explicit, positive verbal feedback is enormously important for women and minorities.[122] The timeliness of constructive criticism is also important.

A communication skill that is important to master from the beginning and even more so as a woman advances up the management ladder is dealing with what one woman at the conference called "jerks" in the organization. Some may be sexist, some are territorially protective, some believe that promotions are based on how many people they supervise. Often these people are in powerful positions, but one can hope to control them with strong management and communication skills.

Self-Confidence

DiTomaso and her colleagues designed a self-assessment model based on the responses of the women they surveyed. Women were less confident in their technological performance and their abilities than are men at comparable levels. In addition, women scientists and engineers were more likely to take direction rather than to set direction. However, this particular study revealed that having a Ph.D. gives women more confidence in their performance and abilities. It also gives them more

---

[121] Jill Wittels, *op. cit.*

[122] Betsy Ancker-Johnson, vice-president of General Motors Corporation (retired), speaking informally at the CWSE conference, Irvine, CA, January 17, 1993.

control in choosing their own work, but it does not have much effect on what kind of work they are assigned.[123]

Successful scientists and managers grow in self-confidence as they learn how to tackle increasingly difficult problems and as others recognize and reward their skills. Women gain recognition and respect for their work by making themselves visible to upper management, making clear the kind of work they do and what special contributions they have to offer as employees.

Self-confidence (not arrogance) is essential. An accumulation of successful outcomes makes self-confidence grow. Self-confidence enables the successful scientist or engineer to take risks, to be a leader, to defend her subordinates, and take the flak if necessary. Self-confidence is important not only in making technical decisions, but also in developing professional relationships.[124]

Deborah Grubbe, engineering manager, Specialty Chemicals, DuPont, summarized the views of several women managers:

> Women who enter management must be comfortable with themselves and have a strong desire to move forward, on their own if necessary. Because the technical management career involves taking risks, both personal and professional, and being responsible for the direction and advancement of other people, women who do this work must be able to face themselves in an honest way and learn where they can improve while maintaining high self-regard. They must be able to ask, "What am I contributing to the situation that is not working?," rather than blaming the other person. They must consider, "How am I helping others, both men and women?" They must maintain personal integrity and consistency of behavior.

As women have gained experience in industry, they have become more realistic about their expectations and aspirations. Women managers are now better able to cope with frustrations than in the past—partly

---

[123] DiTomaso *et al., op. cit.*

[124] *Ibid.*

because they have learned that everyone in industrial management, men and women, experiences ups and downs.

A woman who introduces her comments, either in presentations or conversations, with such statements as "I am not an expert here. . . ." or "I am not sure about this, but. . . ." may unwittingly undermine the competence and confidence she needs to project. A good manager realizes that she does not relinquish responsibility for what she says by using such phrases.[125] On the other hand, she doesn't hesitate to admit not knowing something. She understands that positive, concrete language and direct speech have a powerful influence on others. Her language and communication style need to reflect a high level of self-confidence and the expectation that she will be taken seriously.[126] Further, women scientists and engineers in industry are advised:

> Stay in touch with and trust your instincts. Many men are spending a lot of effort and money trying to learn to do what you already do very successfully. Don't conform to a management style you are not comfortable with.[127]

Openness to Change

Another factor in one's success as a scientist or an engineer is a willingness to change or relocate if necessary. Relocation will not always occur, but change will. One conference speaker talked about the changes in her career, from industry to academe and back, from electrical engineering to computer science, from hands-on research to technical management. Women need to be open to change and not hold on to the idea that they will always be doing the kind of work they did early in their careers.

---

[125] Mary Quade, clinical communications scientist in pharmaceutical research at Parke-Davis, speaking at the CWSE conference, Irvine, CA, January 17, 1993.

[126] Phyllis Mindell, president of Well-Read, cited at the CWSE conference by Leslie Jill Miller of Xerox Corporation.

[127] Jacqueline M. Akinpelu, *op. cit.*

The geographical mobility required in the early career stages seemed to the women interviewed by Anne Preston to be a strong disincentive for women Ph.D. candidates and for women with Ph.D.s who have families to consider.[128] Relocating a spouse and/or children may exact both a high emotional and monetary price. Traditionally, men have accepted their own relocation and its cost to families as the price of advancement. For women the problem is often more difficult, largely because custom does not expect husbands to follow wives. It is reported,

> Many American men feel torn between traditional social
> values and some demands of modern life, but few are
> more brutally torn than those who are following their
> wives as the women ascend the managerial ladder.[129]

However, it is not unusual for women scientists and engineers to relocate as they ascend the corporate ladder:

> Women accounted for about 18% of corporate moves in
> 1992, up from 5% in 1980, the Employee Relocation
> Council says. By the year 2000, some experts say, a third
> of transferees will be female, and one in four trailing
> spouses may be men—up from 15% in 1990 and about
> 7% in 1985.[130]

Many companies recognize the complex issues of relocating families and have made efforts to minimize moves. Lublin reports that Ciba-Geigy, Monsanto, Sprint Corporation, Marriot Corporation, and AT&T are among U.S. companies that have devised "job-aid" packages for "trailing spouses":

> About half of U.S. companies now help relocated mates
> find jobs, usually informally, up from a third in 1986, the

---

[128] Anne Preston, *op. cit.*

[129] Joann S. Lublin, Husbands in limbo, *The Wall Street Journal*, April 13, 1993.

[130] *Ibid.*

Relocation Council says. A common informal approach has been for employers to try to hire spouses themselves or to seek job leads from rivals and suppliers. The number of those with formal programs—such as individualized career counseling, has grown to about 20% from 5% in 1987, estimates relocation consultants Runzheimer International. Impact Group, a St. Louis spouse-counseling firm with special services for trailing husbands, says its list of corporate clients has soared to 71 from 12 in 1989.[131]

General Motors Corporation is another company that has instituted mechanisms to assist spouses of relocated employees, primarily in gaining employment at the new location.

Additional Qualities
of an Effective Manager or Entrepreneur

In addition to the five traits attributed to successful women scientists and engineers in general, three other qualities of effective managers emerged during discussions at the CWSE conference—having a positive attitude, a sense of humor, and a desire to help others. All three were considered outgrowths of one's own strong sense of self, described above. Furthermore, an effective manager must display strength in leadership and in seizing opportunities.

Positive Attitude

Betsy Ancker-Johnson, a former vice-president at General Motors, noted that a manager needs to be upbeat with a "can-do" approach. When confronted with a new situation, a good manager says, "Oh, yes, I've done something like that before." Then she goes off and does it.

Conference participants agreed that taking ownership of and responsibility for one's own career are part of a positive attitude. Women managers must recognize that it is their responsibility to make

---

[131] *Ibid.*

opportunities, to continue to learn new technical material, to keep an open mind, and to ask for help when it is needed.

Sense of Humor

Several speakers noted the importance of a sense of humor for women managers; this includes the ability to take criticism in a good spirit and to express enjoyment in their jobs. Women must be aware that they cannot win every battle. They must look realistically at adverse situations and sometimes diffuse sexist remarks with humor. They should not "take things personally."

A vice-president of engineering shared an experience where she used humor to take the focus off herself and prevent an awkward conflict:

> A few months after my division was bought out, the new corporate science board came to visit and review us. They were mostly consultants who were retired senior military officers. I arrived at the conference room about 10 minutes early, and my boss was already there. He quickly introduced me around the room, and one of the ex-military officers said, "Never had to call a vice-president of engineering 'Jill' before."
>
> I responded without even thinking, "That is the only four-letter word you are allowed to call me today."
>
> Everyone laughed, changed the subject, and on we went. To me, it was one of the times when I really did things right.[132]

Desire To Help Others

Helping others, both women and men, is also an important part of being a manager, whether one is a woman or a man.[133] Supporting one's subordinates is essential to gaining their loyalty, and showing interest in

---

[132] Jill Wittels, *op. cit.*

[133] Barbara Simons, "Women in Computer Science," presentation at the CWSE conference, Irvine, CA, January 17, 1993.

them is not difficult; it just takes time. Criticizing their performance, however, can be difficult. Very few managers are good at sitting down with subordinates individually and explaining something that is faulty or inadequate about their performance. That skill must be developed, and it is essential to success. To have a superior organization, the people in it must excel, and the manager must ensure that they do.

According to Dr. Wittels, good managers are those who have the ability to separate the problems of others from their own:

> They know that because a person is uncomfortable dealing
> with his or her manager does not necessarily mean there is
> something wrong with the manager. Also, good managers
> believe that an employee with a problem is not inherently
> a bad employee; perhaps the person is insecure, immature,
> or having difficulty dealing with change. The good
> manager is one who can find a way to help such a person
> improve his or her performance.

As a manager moves up in the organization, she will know less and less about the details of her subordinates' work. It is essential, however, that she continue to earn their respect and loyalty by appreciating their contributions.[134]

A successful manager will mentor many people, men as well as women, taking the mental stance that part of her purpose is to help those who follow her. She will learn to mentor men and women of all races and ethnic backgrounds; furthermore, she will try to destroy stereotypes.

Leadership

Leadership skills can be learned. Girls are just as adept at leadership as boys at a young age, displaying a natural tendency to lead as they organize games and activities.[135] Girls continue to lead in grammar school through high school as they run for office, organize groups and

---

[134] Betsy Ancker-Johnson, *op. cit.*

[135] Jane Butler Kahle and Marsha Lakes Matyas, *op cit.*

clubs, and exhibit all the basic leadership skills.[136] Leadership opportunities, however, are not offered to women as readily as to men in industry, though some companies are trying to provide equal opportunity.

Leadership development for women is being offered by some professional organizations. At the conference, Catherine J. Didion, executive director of the Association for Women in Science, announced that AWIS plans to organize a conference on leadership skills for women scientists and engineers.

Ability To Seize Opportunities

Women who become successful high-level managers and entrepreneurs have the ability to seize an opportunity and take action. This is quite different from simply being in the right place at the right time. There are always many other people in a particular situation who do not choose to seize an opportunity or do not know how to do this effectively.

An example was presented by Robin Godfrey, a construction cost consultant who was a panelist at the conference session on women entrepreneurs. Working as a secretary for a firm that did construction cost consulting, she saw an opportunity that would benefit the company and made a simple suggestion that turned out to be "an important strategic boon for the company." Ms. Godfrey explained that this opportunity led her to learn the technical skills needed for success in the construction business, which eventually led to the opportunity to buy the business.

Success Factors for the Woman Entrepreneur

Women scientists and engineers who have become successful entrepreneurs also exhibit the key traits that effective women managers do. These are particularly a willingness to take risks, strong leadership skills, an ability to seize opportunities, and a strong managerial style. Successful women entrepreneurs recognize whether they have the necessary skills and strengths to determine if their business plans will be viable. If not, they seek out those who do—mentors, consultants, or employees.

---

[136] Girl Scouts of the U.S.A., *Contemporary Issues: Leading Girls to Mathematics, Science, and Technology,* New York: GSUSA, 1987.

Successful entrepreneurs have singular opportunities. One chief executive officer (CEO) believes that she is more sensitive to the work-family issues of her employees than a man might be. Her company's family leave option is available to both women and men. Another CEO described the positive feeling that most employees experience in her organization. This feeling exists because of the policies that she has established. For instance, all managers in her company have an open door policy, allowing any employee to call to make an appointment or walk in to talk. Training is made available for all employees; vacancies are posted and anyone can apply. There are many team tasks, and the most productive teams have been the ones with a mix of men and women.

Whether they are women or men, successful entrepreneurs (and other high-level managers) often create a corporate culture and a working environment that allow all workers to express their career ambitions to their supervisors.[137] This is especially helpful to women employees, who often wait to be tapped for upward mobility, thinking that their competence is recognized automatically.[138] Men and women should be considered equally for all promotions within a company. In other words, an effective superior is gender and ethnicity blind.

In addition, entrepreneurs must be able to deal with criticism. For example, if the achievements of a woman's company are not getting noticed, she should put the focus on performance results and be very vocal about it. She can demonstrate what is going on in the form of reports, charts, presentations, and so on. In this way, attention is drawn not to herself, but to the performance of her company.

Strategies for Success

There is much to be learned from the many women scientists and

---

[137] Brian Dumaine, The new non-manager manages, *Fortune* **127**(4): 80-84, February 22, 1993.

[138] Women in management, *The Economist* **322**(7752):17-20, 1992; C. Andrew, C. Coderre, and A. Dennis, Stop or go: Reflections of women managers on factors influencing their career development, *Journal of Business Ethics* **9**:361-367, 1990.

engineers whose careers in industrial research and management are successful. The strategies they employ can serve as models for others. Sets of recommendations for individual employees and for managers developed by the Xerox Women's Council are given in Appendix B.

Pamela Atkinson, an engineering education specialist and director of Berkeley's VIEW program in the College of Engineering, has done some qualitative research in which she interviewed 14 women Ph.D.s in electrical engineering and computer science at the University of California, Berkeley. Each subject was asked to talk about her own graduate school experience and was asked what advice she would give to a young woman, just beginning her graduate education, that would help to ensure her success. Some have since entered industry, and others have moved into academe. However, a number of commonalities in their responses apply to successful careers in both industry and academe and led to a list of strategies that women can use in the workplace, as reported by Ms. Atkinson during the CWSE conference:

- Information is worth gold; acquire it and share it.
- Be professionally visible.
- Listen.
- Be aware of your market value.
- Negotiate for what you are worth and believe that it is a lot.
- Develop an important life outside work.
- Don't get into romantic relationships with people you work with.
- Set boundaries on work to protect your outside life.
- Trust your judgment.
- Visualize yourself with power, so that you can address any ambivalence you might feel about wielding it.
- Don't take things personally, even if they are meant that way.
- Intense criticism is worth gold; it provides a lot of information.
- Always look around for other jobs and opportunities.
- A counteroffer from another job is very effective for getting a raise, but only if you are prepared to take the other job.

Many conference participants noted that Ms. Atkinson's list of strategies would be useful for both women and men. One participant opined that women used to be told that "in order to succeed, they must be head and shoulders above men in technical ability" and now are told to be superior at career management, though neither approach addresses the barriers to successful careers for women in science and engineering.[139] However, Jacqueline Akinpelu shared two lessons that she learned during her move up the corporate ladder:

(1)   Although your technical skills played a large part in getting you into management, you now have an expanded arena in which to discover, develop, and extend your skills and interests. Take full advantage of it.

(2)   Realize that, as you gain experience and grow to understand yourself better as a person, your goals may change as well. Stay flexible.

Sometimes in the process of managing, a woman may have to point out to a man unacceptable behavior not related to his job performance. This requires clearly explaining the problem, dispassionately describing alternatives, and finally stating, "This conversation is expected to end the problem." In other words, women in management must sometimes begin an education process with some of the men they work with, including subordinates, counterparts, and superiors. "Not to do so is to abdicate responsibility," according to Betsy Ancker-Johnson, vice-president (retired), General Motors Corporation.

Conference participants suggested strategies for dealing with a hostile manager or a jealous colleague:

- Keep communication alive.
- Develop alternatives that may defuse the hostility.
- Have fun outside work.
- Take jealous hostility as a compliment.
- Stay professional.
- Only go over your manager's head as a last resort.
- Find an impartial, experienced mentor inside or outside the company with whom to discuss work and career-related issues.
- Understand the importance of working in a team.
- Maintain your performance at the highest level.
- Form a network of colleagues, passing along information that will benefit other women.

---

[139] Sheila Pfafflin, district manager of human resources for AT&T, speaking at the CWSE conference, Irvine, CA, January 17, 1993.

It is seen that many common threads run through the various strategies and attributes for success by women scientists and engineers employed in industry. Also there is an overlap with the elements of successful corporate programs discussed in the previous chapters. The insights and experiences that women scientists and engineers were able to share about their careers in industry led participants to formulate a number of strategies to enhance their own successes. The points that were stressed repeatedly were the need for work of the highest possible quality and for developing a balanced personal perspective that recognizes one's own value while giving full support to superiors, peers, and subordinates.

Manuel Fuentes-Cotto, Sheree Lan, and Susan Blackwood discuss the microbending detection feature that alerted monitoring personnel to a potential network outage.
(Photo: AT&T Bell Laboratories)

V. CONCLUSIONS

Women constitute only 12 percent of the S&E work force in industry although they make up 45 percent of the total work force, a trend since 1986. This disparity in large part reflects the fact that women receive fewer S&E degrees than men. Further, women tend to hold degrees in the life sciences, behavioral sciences, and social sciences——fields in which industry traditionally has not been a major employer.

Figures for recent S&E graduates show that a considerably smaller percentage of women than men go into industrial employment. It is also documented that women in industry, at least below the Ph.D. level, are more likely than men (by a factor of about two) to drop out of S&E careers in the early years. The latter two facts suggest that a significant part of the answer to "Why so few?" lies in a less than favorable climate in industry for women scientists and engineers. The major purpose of the conference was to identify ways in which the climate in industry is less favorable to women and ways in which it could be improved. "Why so few?" is also partly the result of women still learning to cope in corporate environments dominated by men.

Conference participants examined many issues, including the influence of cultural and educational background, how women are recruited into industry, working conditions for women scientists and engineers in industry, opportunities for advancement, salaries, and work-family issues. Also discussed were personality traits and actions that women can pursue to enhance their likelihood of success.

The cultural and educational background that leads to relatively few women opting for S&E careers was discussed at the last conference sponsored by the Committee on Women in Science and Engineering (CWSE)[140] and again briefly at this one. It is generally acknowledged that girls and young women experience many negative messages, both from home and school, about pursuing S&E careers.[141] Superimposed on the generally

---

[140] See Marsha Lakes Matyas and Linda Skidmore Dix (eds.), *Science and Engineering Programs: On Target for Women?*, Washington, DC: National Academy Press, 1992.

[141] See, for instance, Jane Butler Kahle and Marsha Lakes Matyas, *op. cit.*

negative image of scientists in this society[142] are views of some people that the goals of women are incompatible with becoming a professional scientist or engineer.[143] Counseling of young women, both by guidance counselors and male S&E professionals, generally does not encourage them to go into S&E careers and may actively discourage them.[144] A frequently stated message is that

> men are inherently more capable of solving scientific and technology-related problems than women. . . . [However,] the mere nature of the subject matter lends itself equally to both males and females, to both young and old, to those who want to become scientists and to those who prefer the humanities.[145]

Nonetheless, one conference participant reported being told, as a minority student, by a male oceanography professor that "women can *only* count plankton."[146] Despite his negative outlook for her, she received a degree in

---

[142] See, for instance, A. J. S. Raye, Researchers embark on effort to improve image of scientists, *The Scientist,* June 22, 1992, pp. 20-21.

[143] See, for instance, Jennifer Wynn, *Perspective: Attracting and Retaining Female Talent,* New York: Catalyst, September 1992; Robert L. Dipboye, "Problems and Progress of Women in Management," in Karen Shallcross Koziara, Michael H. Moskow, and Lucretia Deivey Tanner (eds.), *Working Women: Past, Present, Future,* Washington, DC: The Bureau of National Affairs Inc., 1987.

[144] Douglas L. Friedman, "Minorities in Engineering School: A Data Base for Retention Efforts," NACME Research Letter, New York: National Action Council for Minorities in Engineering (NACME), April 1990.

[145] Yvette Dick Clifton, an Hispanic and African American chemist, presentation at the CWSE conference, Irvine, CA, January 17, 1993.

[146] Catherine Tang, an engineer, speaking at the CWSE conference, Irvine, CA, January 17, 1993.

mechanical engineering and started work in naval architecture but noted "these are the sorts of messages that turn young women away from technological fields." According to the Association of American Colleges,

> . . . some academic advisors underestimate the competence of minority women and thus counsel them to lower their sights or misdirect them on the basis of stereotypes——steering Asian-American women into mathematical and technical fields and Hispanic women into the service and health professions.[147]

These are not uncommon experiences for women, particularly minority women, endeavoring to pursue S&E degrees. However, there is manifestly a wide distribution of talent for science and engineering in both male and female populations. In the best interest of society, it is important to select the most qualified individuals, regardless of gender, ethnic background, race, or other demographic variables.

Stereotyping of behavior and jobs as "male" or "female" poses additional difficulties. Women who try to get into fields or work areas considered "masculine," such as engineering and geoscience, face real discrimination. The commitment to her company of a pregnant woman or a woman with children tends to be questioned, with resultant downgrading of her job responsibilities and promotion opportunities. Nevertheless, a recent study indicates that the organizational commitment of women is nearly identical to that of men, despite the fact that the women in the study felt their companies offered them less opportunity than men.[148]

The origin of many difficulties faced by women in the corporate world is that the workplace generally reflects a male culture. Particularly negative aspects are paternalism, allegations of reverse discrimination, and sexual harassment (more often psychological than physical). Paternalism may result in women not being given jobs or assignments on the grounds that their physical strength is inadequate or the working conditions unsuitable for them. Allegations that the hiring of women is due to affirmative action or corporate quotas can undermine women's self-confidence. Another problem for women

---

[147] Ehrhart and Sandler, *op. cit.*

[148] Arlene Johnson, *op. cit.*

is the perception that they have to work harder than men to prove themselves. Concomitantly, although it is documented that some women are hired at salaries comparable to, or even larger than, those of men with similar background and experiences, the median annual salary for women scientists and engineers is lower than that of men at comparable levels. The situation is even worse for minority women. It should be noted, however, that although the difficulties imposed by the male culture of the workplace are genuine, many women have self-defeating behavior, resulting from low estimates of themselves, low expectations, and low aspirations.

The survey sponsored by the National Science Foundation that documented the greater attrition rate for women scientists and engineers[149] found that their exit rates were highest in the first 10 years of employment. After that the rates began to converge with those of men. Data analysis showed that family status was not the determining factor; the difference in exit rates for women with different family status was small compared to the difference between women and men in the same family status category. Because the attrition of professionals represents a considerable financial loss, some companies make the effort to decrease attrition by improving working conditions for women. In at least one case, Corning, the company was successful over a period of five years in reducing the attrition rate for women to close to that of men. It should be noted that exit rates for Ph.D. women are smaller, close to those for men.

Many companies have set up programs to aid in the recruitment, retention, and advancement of women. Presentations on these programs made by representatives of a number of companies showed many common elements. It was emphasized throughout that the essential underlying element for increasing the number of women in a company and for improving their situation is the commitment of top management.

It is not unusual for industrial recruitment to be carried out by telephone calls to a few chosen colleagues or friends——the old boys' network. To recruit top-quality women and minorities, it is important to make a wider search. Several companies reported summer programs, scholarships, and fellowships as successful recruitment mechanisms. By these means, and regular contacts through specially assigned recruiters, these companies enhanced their success by building relationships with colleges and universities where women and minorities with the desired skills were likely to

---

[149] Anne Preston, *op. cit.*

be found. Another successful tactic rewards employees of a company with a bonus for referring a prospective employee who is subsequently hired.

Many companies have found that corporate women's networks and advocacy groups have an important positive influence on recruitment and retention of women, providing a support system. Such a network can carry out mentoring and make suggestions to management on work-family issues or how to deal with sexual harassment, for example. It was emphasized that for the network to be successful, and to be viewed as an asset by management, its relevance to the bottom line should be clearly stated.

The conference participants generally agreed that mentoring is of great importance. Research shows that women with successful S&E careers, almost without exception, had mentors who supported and encouraged them, particularly through the early phase of their careers. One company has institutionalized mentoring to the extent that each new female employee is given a mentor who is responsible for teaching the protegé how to progress in the company, encouraging her to take risks, and fully supporting her with appropriate training. To ensure the success of the mentorship program in this company, the mentors are given financial rewards, compensatory time, and other incentives. Another program found valuable by some companies is confidential one-on-one counseling, which is also made available to men.

According to a recent survey of scientists and engineers in a few large technical companies, neither men nor women give their companies high marks for career development. The situation could be improved by following the recommendations of the Xerox Corporation's Women's Council:

- the criteria for promotion should be clarified;
- job opportunities throughout the company should be publicized; and
- internal hiring opportunities should be created to promote inter-organizational flow.

The latter two measures are particularly important at a time when companies are not growing or, in fact, are shrinking. It was noted that lateral transfers may be important for subsequent promotion, but many women tend to avoid these transfers, apparently regarding them as risky. Whether or not this is the case, the glass ceiling is still a reality. Despite significant increases in the number of women in management in some companies, 95 percent of the top executive jobs in industry are held by white males. It might be argued that there have not been enough women in the pipeline in industry long enough for a sizable number to have achieved top status. However, in the cases of medicine, investment banking, and accounting, where sufficient numbers of women have been in the field long enough, the numbers in the top ranks remain much smaller than would be implied by the pipeline model. Still, some companies are making a special effort to find qualified women and to promote them. An effective way of achieving this is to make managers' performance appraisals dependent in part on their success in hiring and promoting women. Salary inequities between men and women also are being addressed by some companies.

Seeing clearly that maximum productivity of all employees is best for the bottom line, some companies are attempting to improve the climate for women and to remove obstacles to their performance by "sensitivity training." One company shows groups of employees, including managers at all levels, videos made by professional actors portraying undesirable behavior toward women that has occurred within the group. Another type of effort for improving the climate is providing role models. In this respect, minority women have been less fortunate, minority role models in science and engineering being even scarcer than for white women.

Work-family issues are of paramount importance; how a company addresses these issues has a great effect on its ability to retain women scientists and engineers. Paid maternity leave of six weeks or more, plus the possibility of unpaid leave beyond that, is offered by some companies. Two companies reported lactation facilities for the use of nursing mothers. Because, as many studies indicate, the major responsibility for child and dependent care and household chores still falls largely on women, it is important for companies to have options for part-time work and some flexibility in working hours. Many women stressed that taking advantage of the option for part-time work, however, carries a stigma, jeopardizing future advancement. In addition to destigmatizing part-time work, companies should be flexible about allowing employees to take time off for sick children and other family emergencies. Part-time and flexible arrangements are particularly important because women who leave for a time, due to dependent care or other problems, find it difficult to return to science and engineering, and are thus forced to begin new occupations.[150]

Some companies provide on-site day care for children. Others have taken leadership roles in developing community initiatives to improve the supply and quality of child care. Where the latter is not considered a problem, as in large communities, a company might provide referrals to

---

[150] *Ibid.*

child-care facilities. A helpful trend recently found in some companies is "cafeteria benefits," or the tailoring of a benefits package to the needs of the individual.

Another important work-family issue is that of dual-career couples. Some companies still will not hire two family members, even in different departments. A helpful approach, if only one spouse is hired, is for the company to provide active assistance in finding a job for the other.

Discussion at the conference also focused on attitudes and strategies for women to achieve successful careers in industry. Five attributes appear to be common to women (and men) who have successfully pursued industrial careers in science and engineering:

(1)   technical expertise and competence;
(2)   ability to establish goals and take risks;
(3)   strong communication skills, including the ability to express the desire for a promotion and to deal tactfully with men having negative attitudes about women in the workplace;
(4)   self-confidence; and
(5)   openness to change.

To achieve successful careers in industry, women scientists and engineers were advised to (1) set objectives, (2) meet performance requirements, (3) know their organization, and (4) seek opportunities for self-development. A complementary set of recommendations for managers of women scientists and engineers in industry emphasized communication of what is required for corporate and individual success and for support of employees' career planning and professional development. Successful managers, in addition to the five traits listed above, should have a positive or "can-do" attitude, a sense of humor, and a desire to help others. It was noted that management skills can be learned, much as technical skills are. Women in management can and should use their power and influence to improve the situation for other women.

More and more S&E women, frustrated by the constricted opportunities and obstacles they found in industry, have become entrepreneurs. Successful entrepreneurship requires, in addition to the attributes mentioned above, strong leadership skills, which can be learned, and the ability to seize an opportunity and take action. It was agreed, however, that entrepreneurship is not for everyone.

Minority women in industry by and large suffer more discrimination than white women. Their cultural backgrounds often pose additional barriers to an S&E career than is the case for white women. Nevertheless, it was the consensus of conference participants that minority women are strengthened by retaining their ethnic and cultural heritage.

In these volatile economic times, some programs to recruit and advance women have been curtailed. It is important to remember, however, that, particularly in the international competitive race in which we now find ourselves, it is essential to employ the best talent, whatever the gender or race. In suggesting the steps that might be taken by participants in U.S. industry——individual scientists and engineers, their managers, and CEOs of corporations——the Committee concurs with the assessments of several conference participants:

> *What benefits women usually benefits men. What we need to do is show how these changes make sense for us as a society.* [151]

However,

> *Society cannot change until people change, [but] change is an important page in the manual for the survival of women in industry. Equality can only be achieved as both men and women are emancipated from the past and willingly reject traditional beliefs, values, and methods.* [152]

---

[151] Catherine J. Didion, executive director of the Association for Women in Science (AWIS), speaking at the CWSE conference, Irvine, CA, January 17, 1993. For more information about AWIS, contact Ms. Didion at 1522 K Street NW, Suite 820, Washington, DC 20005.

[152] Paula Graham, *op. cit.*

APPENDIX A:
APPROACHING CHANGE[153]

Linda S. Wilson

The Context

We are here to explore why industry employs and advances so few women as scientists and engineers. We conduct our inquiry in the context of an environment that is beset with rapid and seemingly constant change. These changes are not minor incremental adjustments. They are changes of significant proportion. They are fundamental transformations and realignments, and they are shaping the parameters within which social, political, and economic events will unfold for many years to come.

I will not dwell on these changes. You have heard about them in speech after speech for the past year or so. Terms like global interdependence, economic competitiveness, and "new world order" have become part of our daily lexicon, and we know that they have profound consequences for how Americans conduct business and view national security.

There are also growing complexities and urgencies regarding how we deal with human rights around the world and human welfare at home. There are fundamental shifts in the roles of federal and state governments and in the relationships among government, universities, and industry. There is a clear recognition that, while developments in science and technology exert great influence on our lives, many of our citizens are woefully illiterate in these disciplines.

So this is the context of swirling change in which we find ourselves as a new century, indeed a new millennium, approaches. While nothing

---

[153] This chapter is adapted from a presentation given by Dr. Wilson at the conference——"Women Scientists and Engineers Employed in Industry: Why So Few?"——in Irvine, CA, January 17, 1993.

magical will occur at midnight on December 31, 1999, our vision of that date on the horizon is a useful focal point around which we can galvanize our energy and ideas, reflect upon where we have been, reexamine and rethink our priorities, and plan for the future. With this in mind, the Office of Scientific and Engineering Personnel has moved from a year-to-year planning process to a more strategic, longer-term approach——that is, to projecting human resource needs and planning how to meet them.

Human resources are vital to progress in science and technology, and in a competitive global economy, we cannot afford to ignore or squander them. Women and minority groups are substantially underrepresented in science and engineering. They are resources upon which we need to draw more heavily. This becomes clear when we look at changing demographics and recognize that talent is distributed widely among segments of the population.

It also becomes clear, as the Committee on Women in Science examines what is happening to women in these fields, that we need to focus some specific attention on women in industry. We want to know why, in many U.S. industries, so few women scientists and engineers are employed and why their progress seems to be slower than that of men. In conducting our inquiry, we should learn many important things about women and about industry.

We should also learn about basic human motivation. This is something we do not understand very well, and we are paying the consequences. The costs of our ignorance are enormous, whether we measure them in drug abuse, delinquency, crime, violence, or in many other ways. At my own institution, Harvard and Radcliffe, faculty from a number of departments are undertaking some new coordinated research on the topic "brain, mind, and behavior." One important focus of their work will be human motivation. I am confident that what they learn will help us understand the kinds of issues that concern us here today. And I am hopeful that what we learn here will be helpful in other areas.

Against this backdrop I want to accomplish several things this morning. First, I will quickly review the compelling arguments for the full participation of women in industry and in other sectors. Then I will identify some recurring themes you are likely to hear over the next two days. This will provide a context——a kind of intellectual map——that I hope will help you process the large volume of information that will be presented. I will then proceed to identify some underlying issues that we need to look at very, very closely. And I will conclude by reporting briefly on some recent research conducted by visiting scholars at Radcliffe College.

Compelling Arguments

Why should society remove barriers that inhibit full participation by women in industry and in many other areas of our society? There are two basic arguments. The first argument is that equal opportunity is a matter of social justice, that all citizens are entitled to fair and equitable treatment. This is a simple argument and one that should be sufficient in and of itself.

The second argument is that increasing the number of trained and engaged women scientists and engineers in industry is an economic imperative. By the end of the decade, women and minorities will constitute a majority of the net new entrants to the work force. Our ability to compete in a global economy, which means our economic security, will be determined in large measure by how well we train these people and the extent to which society utilizes their talents.

A corollary of this argument is that women and minorities bring to the workplace different perspectives and experiences that provide important sources of the renewal and resilience needed during a period of transition and change. Some of the adjustments that are necessary to secure a sustainable future, in contrast to the technology and arms races in which we have been engaged, will require the public's willingness to make short-term sacrifices for the long-term good. Women and minorities must be part of that long-term commitment.

As we consider these arguments——one based on social justice and the other on comparative economic advantage——it should be clear that they are mutually compatible. Indeed, they are interdependent in the long run.

115

Recurring Themes

Let me turn now to four recurring themes from the literature and news media that are likely to be raised during the course of this conference:

(1)   Complexity in the participants' culture

Like men who are scientists or engineers, women scientists and engineers as a group are not monolithic. They come from different cultures, were trained at different institutions, work in different organizations, and perform different roles within those organizations. The information we develop by identifying these differences will, I believe, point to the convergence of some indicators that can help us partially to understand why there are so few women in science and engineering in industry.

In examining the cultural dimensions of the issue, we must be very careful not to be blinded by Eurocentric biases. Very real differences exist in the culture and the demography of this country today. To succeed in the future, we must understand and value these differences and learn to accommodate them.

The socialization process within ethnic groups involves learning cultural values as well as gender roles. When we consider women of color, we must be careful to recognize the very real double jeopardy they may experience. In the case of African American women, we need to bear in mind that they are traditionally expected to protect men. In Asian cultures, women are expected to support their organizations, and, generally speaking in American culture, women have been expected to place a high value on personal relationships and to be rather careful about being assertive or aggressive.

(2)   Complexity in the processes

Multiple factors influence women's career paths. These factors include opportunity, achievement, and choice, and they are connected to each other.

A relatively recent report on women in the chemical industry[154] provides some useful information about the shortage of women in that field. The report also suggests some explanations for the way in which women progress. These explanations are hypotheses and not definite conclusions. One suggestion is that gender differences exist in scientific ability——that men are naturally better at science than women. This is a questionable hypothesis, but, nonetheless, one that is on the table.

A second suggestion is that gender differences arise from social attitudes and self-selection by women. Because discrimination has existed against women in chemistry over the years, women have been reluctant to enter that field. And because there are so few females in chemistry, the view persists that this is not an appropriate field for women. Self-selection of a more general nature also may be at work. Faced with the consequences of marriage and motherhood, women have tended to steer away from chemistry and other sciences. The result has been an accumulation of advantages for some and disadvantages for others. Throughout the process, certain groups, in this case men, receive greater resources, while nonrecipient groups, in this case women, become relatively impoverished. This is true even in the absence of intentional discrimination.

This is sometimes called a triple penalty or an interconnected set of relationships: the cultural attitude that science is an inappropriate field for women leads to discrimination; discrimination leads to a reduction in the motivation of women workers; and loss of motivation leads to reduction in women's performance. All of this combined leads to withdrawal from careers, obsolescence of skills, and a further reduction in opportunities. It is a chain of interrelated factors that plays itself out, in one way or another, in many different fields.

(3)   U.S. culture, social dynamics, and the sociology of learning

For a very long time, the socialization process has taught men to be good providers. We see this in surveys of men's views of masculinity that

---

[154] Corinne Marasco, "A Manly Profession: Women in Chemistry," *Workforce Report*, Washington, DC: American Chemical Society, May 1991.

have been conducted over the course of many years. The primary definition of masculinity that emerges from these surveys is being a good provider. The notion that men are responsible for being good providers is deeply embedded in our culture, and it reinforces the structures that exist in industry, academe, government, and other organizations. These structures produce and reflect patterns of behavior that are absent or discouraged in women. As more women participate in the game and move up the organizational ladder, they must learn to play by the existing rules before they can change or adapt them to their talents and culture.

Let me cite an example from the work of Gerald Holton, a faculty member at Harvard. He did a study of the number of scientific articles published by women.[155] He found that women tend to publish fewer papers than men but that the papers are longer and more comprehensive. Women seem to take paper writing very seriously, while men tend to develop their careers by publishing shorter, less comprehensive work. Since men are more prevalent in science than women, their behavior tends to establish the norm for what is expected in the field. And since papers and publications are among the most important tangible products upon which scientists are evaluated, you can see how the differences in the way people approach their publications can produce different career outcomes. To clarify the point, one could say that women focus primarily on conducting science (or at least more so than men) while men give more focus to developing their careers. Men do this not for any crass motive, but because society, through acculturation, has taught them they must be good providers. The same responsibility has not been assigned to women historically. This is now changing as women enter the work force in greater numbers, not simply out of a passion to do science but for economic reasons as well.

In considering the social dynamics that apply in the business culture, it is important to take note of the five Rs that describe what is expected of

---

[155] Gerald Holton and Gerhardt Sonnert, *Project Access: A Study of Access of Women Scientists and Engineers to Research Careers*, Boston: Harvard University, March 18, 1991.

people in business.[156] These five Rs are respect (both earned and given), responsibility, resourcefulness, revenue development (or "rain making"), and risk taking. Women are a part of this culture only to the extent that they explicitly embrace and deal with the five Rs. Until one is part of that culture and successful, it is very hard to make it adapt.

(4)   Change

It is important to reframe and restructure organizations and to redefine and redistribute roles of men and women. Expectations and relationships are changing, and it is all a bit unsettling. It is unsettling especially for those who have been in the majority, in part because of larger transformations that are under way. In addressing these issues, however, one must remember that we are dealing with a basic culture and set of expectations (like the need to be a good provider) that are deeply ingrained. The sand is now shifting and security is diminished. The stakes are very high. The issue is not simply enabling women to make their way. It is getting men and women and the organizations within which they work to engage in mutual adaptation.

These, then, are the four themes I expect to unfold as the conference proceeds——complexity in the participants' culture, complexity in processes, the culture itself, and change.

Underlying Issues

Let us turn our attention now to some underlying issues that we extract from these four themes.

Power: Shared and not shared

What, we must ask, sets science and engineering apart from other lines of work? What is it about science and engineering that historically has

---

[156] Dawn-Marie Driscoll and Carol R. Greenberg, *Membership in the Club: The Coming of Age of Executive Women*, New York: Free Press, forthcoming 1993.

119

allowed our society to view them as being inappropriate for women? What has become so ingrained in our culture that even today we call science and engineering "nontraditional" occupations for women?

Is it an association society perceives between science and engineering and military and destructive purposes?

Was it the early and widely held beliefs that women's intellects were much less developed than men's and that they were incapable of undertaking science and mathematics? Do not forget that as recently as the turn of the century scholars believed that women's brains were much smaller than men's and that their intellects were akin to those of children and chimpanzees. It was also believed that if women used their minds extensively, their reproductive ability would suffer. Perhaps this has had something to do with society's view that women should stay away from science and engineering.

Or perhaps it was a belief that women's subordinate social status was inconsistent with a passion to question, discover, and push the boundaries of knowledge.

It is important to probe the relationship between the historical reasons why women were excluded from science and engineering and the power dynamics that are in play today because such connections can be very deeply embedded in our culture. When this happens it becomes difficult to bring about change. As we look at what is happening both in this country and in other countries, both developed and underdeveloped, we may more easily discover what we can do to change this situation.

The system within which our science and engineering enterprises operate

This system has some fundamental flaws. It has proved to be very resistant to adaptation in order to include women. This is a value judgment. Some would say it has adjusted very rapidly as the overall social system has changed. After all, the major push did not begin until 20 to 25 years ago. On the other hand, those in the system who have watched changes in other areas feel that progress in these fields has been rather slow. The point is arguable.

The system of science and engineering enterprises has also dealt very inadequately, some would say not at all, with the need to develop effective ways to recycle human capital resources——ways, for example, to reclaim and renew the talents of people who have left the work force for one reason or another. This has been especially true in regard to women, who, incidentally, constitute half the population.

When women bear children they must stop work momentarily and sometimes longer. They must also deal with the responsibility that our society continues to impose on them to carry the brunt of the burden of raising children. At the same time that economic pressures today require that women work, our system has built no bridges to enable them to return to the workplace and regain momentum——none, that is, but the most rickety of bridges.

The patchwork quilt of women's careers is a testimony to their ingenuity in dealing with this fundamental flaw in our system.

So, with those four themes and two issues on the table, I submit to you that the challenge we face is the need for mutuality of adaptation among men and women and work organizations. How these issues relate goes to the very heart of the matter. How they are negotiated and resolved will have a tremendous impact on the quality of the working environment and our ability to build a sustainable future.

One way to approach thinking about these issues of power and adaptation is to ask ourselves why women scientists and engineers, particularly those holding the Ph.D., appear to do better in academe than in industry. I must add, as an aside, that I would be among the first to say that universities too have not done a very good job on this front. Nevertheless, differences do exist in the numbers of women in the two sectors and how well they progress.

One can quickly suggest a number of reasons, and I won't attempt to provide an exhaustive list. I will give just a few that may be illustrative. The greater flexibility in the work schedule in academia may very well be a part of it, and the role that students play in universities may be important too in that the number of women attending colleges and universities has increased greatly since the 1960s. This expansion may have enabled the social system to change more rapidly on campuses than in industry, which has remained male-dominated.

Another part of the explanation may be the greater decentralization of authority in academe. The short-term horizon and bottom-line driving force in industry may have deterred women from participating. They do not come with the built-in cultural requirement to be good providers that is a large part of the driving force for men.

The more frequent use of teams in industry may be a paradox of sorts. The initial barriers to acceptance of women (or most often one woman) into a team may have a lot to do with the difficulty of "getting in and getting on with it" in industry in the early career stage. In academe it may be easier for women to pursue their ideas, since the work is more individualized. At the same time, we find in academe that the isolation of women in the sciences impedes their progression to seniority. Some of the social supports and collaborative learning that takes place in teams are often not available to women in higher education.

The increasing number of dual-career couples and the need to be mobile also suggest themselves as reasons why women prefer academic employment to working in industry, in that greater opportunities to accommodate dual-career couples may exist in large cities with multiple institutions of higher learning.

Please do not get me wrong: universities have a long way to go. But the preference that women have shown for universities over industry is real, and it holds some potential for helping us to understand what is happening.

Metaphors To Stimulate Understanding and Communication

With these two issues, and that set of themes, let me now suggest some metaphors that may be useful in understanding and communicating the underparticipation of women in the industrial work force of the United States. Let me also caution you to use the metaphors very carefully, lest they limit or misdirect your thinking.

One interesting metaphor was developed by Gerhardt Sonnert of Harvard, who worked with Gerald Holton on that study of women's publication rates I mentioned earlier.[157] Sonnert talks about the need that women have to synchronize three clocks——their biological clock, their career clock, and their spouse's clock. It is, in a way, a triple threat and a triple burden.

Another very useful metaphor is that of critical mass, a term that is widely used in science and engineering. I think it was Mildred Dresselhaus who helped us begin to apply that concept to career development and advancement for women, especially in education. She showed us how the dynamics of a classroom change when women become at least 15 percent of the group.

What we need to do, then, is to recognize that the adaptation I have called for will come about more easily as more women move into the work force and as they become distributed more evenly.

A third metaphor we have heard so much about is the glass ceiling. It is important to recognize that this one can be limited and should be used with great caution. It has, like many metaphors, the advantage of two words and a clear mental image that holds out some hope while acknowledging some frustrations. But I think we have gone beyond some of the early work on this concept and have a deeper understanding of what is happening on the other side of the ceiling. We understand that, in fact, the ceiling may not be imposed from above. That is why I say it is important to be careful about the use of metaphors.

Let me add two more metaphors to the array. One is that of the lattice. As I work in this area I have to remind myself continually that we are dealing with a system that has many interconnected parts and that, unfortunately, most of the participants in the system do not think about it as a system. They focus on their own particular part and what they can do to optimize results for themselves and others in their neighborhood. But if we think of the issue as a lattice of interconnected objects with flexible bonds between them, we can see that we cannot touch any one part without causing reverberations throughout the system. As we try to make sense of this system and improve it fairly rapidly, it is important that all participants

---

[157] Holton and Sonnert, *op. cit.*

understand this interconnectedness and appreciate the larger context in which they exist.

The final metaphor I want to leave you with is that of the reservoir. It is not original with me, but I think it is helpful. In the last 20 years we have moved away from thinking of science and technology as operating on a linear model in which basic research generates ideas, ideas generate applications, and applications generate products. We understand now (although we sometimes act as though we do not) that this is not the way the system works. Basic research is not really the beginning of a long pipeline but, rather, a reservoir into which one can dip to get a better understanding of how and why things work. We now know that many of the driving forces in technology and product development come from outside basic research.

Current Research

Now that we have taken a quick look at both the power and the limitations of metaphors, let us move on to the final portion of my talk, which deals with some current research. I want to tell you about the work of two different types of scholars.

The first is Bernadette Nelson, who is a consultant in a firm that serves manufacturing and service companies and who is visiting us right now at Radcliffe College. She is working closely with corporations as they try to deal with the changing demography and cope with the diversification of their work forces. She has been working with the management of companies and also in focus groups, training managers to recognize and value the differences that diversity brings, and helping them to build a more cohesive work force.

She reports[158] that attrition among women in industry is very high, that most leave their jobs within 1-5 years. The difficulty lies not in attracting women in the first place. The difficulty is getting the young women who are hired to stay on the job. Companies are deeply concerned about this, but they do not understand what it is happening. What is happening, according to Nelson, is that women do not receive appropriate

---

[158] Bernadette Nelson, personal communication, January 1993.

recognition for their work, they are not advancing in their positions, and they are struggling mightily to balance the demands of work and family. Companies are recruiting some of the best and the brightest, and they think they are treating men and women the same, which is not totally true. In any event, the system is not responding as intended.

Her analysis of this is that men are coming into a system that functions well for them, whereas women are not. The chemical industry, she reports, is feeling this acutely. The women feel that they are beating their heads against a brick wall. Men are stressed in these companies, too, especially the young men with wives who are leaving jobs because of tension. Some of these men as well as women are opting to get off the fast track.

The message we derive from this is that, in some way, work has to be restructured to accommodate today's work force. In this restructuring, we will change people and we will change organizations. But in the end what we will really do is change our view of work and our understanding of how it functions. We will restructure work itself, and it is useful to see the issue this way.

The need to accommodate a diverse work force is only one of the reasons why our approach to work needs to change. Other factors include the downsizing of the work force and the need to work in a much more interdependent environment. In point of fact, the basic compact that has governed the workplace for many years is now being challenged. In the past the compact in industry stated that workers would work hard, the whole family would support the worker, and industry would take care of the worker. Mutual loyalty between employer and worker was very functional. But with the changing economic climate and the restructuring of industry, worker loyalty is no longer being repaid; the compact is coming unglued. What seems to be required is a new kind of flexibility and career path, both for the sake of organizations and the sake of those who work in them.

Let me turn now to my other colleagues, Dawn-Marie Driscoll and Carol Goldberg, who have been studying women in management in a broad range of fields, including law, business, industry, and education.[159] They

---

[159] Driscoll and Goldberg, *op. cit.*

125

have been identifying the factors that contributed to the success of these women and the strategies that they have used to get ahead.

One of the factors associated with success that they have identified is "rain making," or the ability to generate business. I spoke about this briefly at the start of my talk. Women often have not understood that in the business world they cannot just work hard, do a good job, and go home. They are expected to bring in business. Think for a moment about a lawyer. It is one thing to be extremely knowledgeable and effective in the courtroom, but if you do not bring in clients, and cannot develop the clients, the law firm does not flourish. The socialization process has bestowed this rain-making function on men and equipped them to play this role later in life. By and large rain making has not been part of the socialization of women.

A second factor that has contributed to the success of women has been their ability to counter cultural stereotypes about themselves by developing professional visibility and personal currency, forging friendships with male peers, and combating subtle sexism. As for the strategies that successful women use, Driscoll and Goldberg have identified several. They include developing leadership skills in women's networking organizations, assuming active roles in mainstream businesses and organizations, and thereby influencing the development of social and economic policy. In other words, these women engaged not just narrowly in their work setting, but in the larger community context, in places where power and influence are wielded.

This research suggests an approach to change——a goal really—— that I would like to leave with you. Driscoll and Goldberg call the goal "partnership feminism," by which they mean men and women working together to improve the economic status of all citizens. It is a strategy that combines feminist values of care and interdependence with the realities of world economics and productivity in a partnership in which neither sex dominates.

APPENDIX B
RELATED TABLES

TABLE B-1: Recommendations to Individual Scientists and Engineers

Category	Action
Set Objectives	Identify and communicate your personal objectives. Test reality with managers, peers, counselors, and mentors. Understand total requirements and market value of the job.
Meet Performance Requirements	Excel both in performance and interpersonal skills. Effect team collaboration. Be a role model or mentor to others. Take steps to ensure your internal scientific visibility and stature, via reports, presentations, and invited talks. Ensure your external scientific visibility and stature (publications, presentations, invited talks, patents, professional society activities).
Know Your Organization	Understand your organization and the strategic intent of the business. Comprehend technology directions. Assess research priorities and technical activities to leverage your expertise.
Seek Development Opportunities	Increase the breadth of your skills. Participate in both formal training (internally and externally) and cross-functional and cross-organizational experiences. Be prepared to relocate. Seek ongoing advice and feedback. Engage in academic outreach and university interactions. Seek opportunities for project management. Seek and leverage external funding.

SOURCE: Presentation of Leslie Jill Miller, Xerox Corporation, at the CWSE conference, Irvine, CA, January 17, 1993.

TABLE B-2: Recommendations to Managers of Scientists and Engineers in Industry

Category	Action
Communicate	Emphasize: Organizational goals and activities Standards of excellence and relevance Critical core competencies and skills required for personal and business success Ongoing honest and timely feedback
Proactively Support Career Planning	Engage in regular objective setting. Discuss multiyear career goals annually. Follow through with Development Action Plans. Initiate career development discussions. Provide information and advice regarding career development actions, options, and training. Encourage educational opportunities, including sabbaticals. Support the writing of papers and attendance at conferences. Enable individuals to maintain internal and external scientific visibility.
Set Up and Support Development Opportunities	Champion your people and assist them toward their development goals. Create opportunities for internal visibility. Foster cross-organizational and cross-discipline opportunities. Provide cross-training for promotion and job satisfaction. Provide project management opportunities. Recommend candidates for internal and external opportunities. Work to remove barriers to publication.

SOURCE: Presentation of Leslie Jill Miller, Xerox Corporation, at the CWSE conference, Irvine, CA, January 17, 1993.